The Book of Stars

The Book of Stars

By Ancient The Architect

"In the heart of all creation lies the spark of divine understanding; to know oneself is to know the universe, for each soul is a mirror reflecting the infinite wisdom of the cosmos."

Copyright and Disclaimer

Copyright © 2024 Ancient The Architect

All rights reserved. No part of this book may be reproduced, distributed, or transmitted in any form or by any means, including photocopying, recording, or other electronic or mechanical methods, without the prior written permission of the publisher, except in the case of brief quotations in critical reviews and certain other noncommercial uses permitted by copyright law.

This copyright covers all written material within the book, the book cover design, and any original interpretations or concepts presented throughout.

ISBN: 9798992210200

Disclaimer

The contents of this book are intended for informational and educational purposes only. They reflect the author's interpretations and insights based on ancient philosophies, metaphysical traditions, and spiritual perspectives. This work should not be considered as offering definitive statements but rather as an exploration for readers to reflect upon.

The author and publisher make no representations regarding the accuracy or completeness of the information and are not responsible for any conclusions or actions taken based on the book's content. Readers are encouraged to conduct their own research and consult additional sources on spiritual and metaphysical matters.

Published by Health Is Luxury

Table of Contents

1st Entry: Introduction — *Pg. 1*

- *Setting the Stage for a Metaphysical Journey*

2nd Entry: The Yuga Cycles — *Pg. 5*

- *Understanding Cosmic Time and Spiritual Evolution*

3rd Entry: Ancient Egyptian Metaphysical Profiles of the Gods — *Pg. 10*

- ***Archetypes of Divine Qualities***
- ***Nu:*** *The Primordial Waters of Creation*
- ***Shu:*** *The Energy of Air and Space*
- ***Hetep:*** *The Essence of Peace and Rest*
- ***Ma'at:*** *The Principle of Universal Balance and Truth*
- ***Thoth:*** *The Keeper of Wisdom and Sacred Knowledge*
- ***Imhotep:*** *The Architect of Healing and Intelligence*
- ***Ptah:*** *The Divine Creator and Master Builder*
- ***Hathor:*** *The Emanation of Joy, Love, and Beauty*
- ***Nephthys:*** *The Protector of Mystical Transition*
- ***Anubis:*** *The Guide of Souls and Transformation*
- ***Set:*** *The Catalyst of Chaos and Necessary Change*
- ***Isis:*** *The Divine Mother and Nurturer of Magic*
- ***Horus:*** *The Warrior and Visionary of Higher Sight*
- ***Osiris:*** *The Archetype of Regeneration and Resurrection*
- ***Ra:*** *The Embodiment of Divine Light and Power*
- ***Amen:*** *The Hidden One, Source of Infinite Potential*

4th Entry: The 12 Tribes of Israel as Mental Qualities — *Pg. 136*

- *Foundational Aspects of the Spiritual Mind*

5th Entry: Apostles vs. Disciples: A Metaphysical Exploration — *Pg. 149*

- *The Apostolic Chakra Guide*
- *Exploring the 12 Apostles/Disciples Metaphysically*

6th Entry: Christ Hood: The Path of Jesus in Metaphysical Terms — *Pg. 225*

- *Embarking on the Path to Spiritual Mastery*

7th Entry: The Sun of God in the Metaphysical Framework — *Pg. 238*

- *Enhanced with Hindu Metaphysical Perspectives*
- *The Second Coming: Integration of the Lower and Higher Self*
- *The Messiah as the Living Breath of Truth and Love*
- *Galilee: The Path of Spiritual Progress and Resurrection*

8th Entry: Archangels, Cherubim and Seraphim, Elohim: Guardians of Divine Wisdom and Higher Realms — *Pg. 246*

- *The Role of the Archangels*
- *Seraphim - Guardians of the Buddhi Plane*
- *Cherubim - Guardians of Divine Knowledge*
- *The Elohim - Custodians of Divine Will*

9th Entry: Celestial Wisdom: The Zodiac as the Cosmic Path of the Soul — *Pg. 260*

- *The Twelve Stages of the Zodiac: A Journey of Mental Qualities*
- *Complete Metaphysical Exploration of Each Zodiac Sign*
- *Practical Cyclic Exercises*

1st Entry

Introduction: The Journey from Son of Man to Sun of God

This book is an invitation, a gateway into the depths of your being and the mysteries of existence. It does not merely acknowledge the presence of a soul but urges you to become conscious of its essence, to understand its nature, and to uncover the radiant inner sun that lies within. This journey is not a simple traversal; it is an alchemical transformation, a passage from the son of man—the human bound to earthly experience—to the Sun of God, the divine light that exists both beyond and within all things.

The son of man is that part of us still intertwined with earthly desires, the mind yet bound by the limitations of ego and form. It represents the evolving aspect of consciousness striving toward higher realms. The Sun of God, however, is the symbol of our divine inheritance, the luminous Self that transcends duality, eternally present within each being. This text seeks to guide you through this profound transformation, illuminating the path with ancient wisdom and practical insight.

In this journey, we must speak of symbology—the language of wisdom. True wisdom is not linear or one-dimensional; it flows from the higher mind, where every symbol holds layered meanings within it. The grand architecture of existence is mirrored in the 360 degrees of the zodiac cycle, itself a symbolic circumscription of universal knowledge. Each of the 12 signs within this cycle serves as a gateway, offering insight into our progression as microcosms of the universe itself. As you engage with these symbols, you are invited to expand, becoming more invisible in ego yet more powerful in essence, shifting from mere human awareness to divine consciousness.

At the heart of this evolution is the Christ Principle—the awakening of the inner Christ within each of us. The Christ Principle is the Atma-Buddhi, the spiritual essence representing divine wisdom and love. As the soul refines and transcends the lower qualities, this inner Christ emerges. This transformation is more than passive awareness; it is the active embodiment of divine truth and compassion. The Christ within is the Sun of God, the eternal light guiding each step of the journey from unawareness to awareness, from darkness to light, from a state of degeneration to regeneration.

In these pages, you will encounter the metaphysical profiles of the 12 disciples, who represent stages in our spiritual journey and the qualities that emerge along the way. Each disciple embodies a distinct virtue, providing a model for understanding how our inner struggles and aspirations echo the universal path toward enlightenment. This journey of discipleship is deeply connected to the symbolism of the 12 tribes of Israel. Each of the 12 tribes signifies a unique mental quality—a metaphysical attribute within the mind.

When these qualities are cultivated and disciplined, they transform into discipleship, evolving into embodiments of divine consciousness that guide the soul toward its highest purpose.

Moreover, this book delves into the wisdom of the ancient Egyptian gods, not as mere mythological figures but as archetypal forces that reflect universal principles within us. Through a metaphysical lens, we honor these gods as embodiments of cosmic energies and spiritual truths that resonate within the soul, awaiting our recognition and integration. Their symbols and stories are here to serve as mirrors, reflecting deeper truths about our own inner divinity and the timeless path of transformation.

The zodiac signs, likewise, are presented not as simple astrological symbols but as phases within the larger cosmic and personal cycles of life. Each sign within the zodiac offers a stage in the evolution of the soul, inviting us to contemplate its wisdom and align with the universal rhythms it represents. Included are contemplative practices meant to deepen your connection to these energies, harmonizing your spirit with the cyclical flow of the cosmos.

While we briefly touch upon the Yuga cycles from ancient Vedic knowledge, our primary focus remains on integrating and practically applying these teachings to daily life. This book invites you to engage with these truths not as abstract concepts but as living principles that can transform your mind, heart, and spirit.

Together, these elements form a structured framework of spiritual insight, offering a roadmap for the soul's ascent. This work is a call to awaken the divine essence within, to see beyond the illusions of the material world, and to embrace the eternal truth that we are both human and divine. The Christ Principle shines as a guiding beacon, urging us not merely to reflect divine attributes but to embody the indwelling Christ—the essence of love, wisdom, and unity.

The journey of spiritual evolution also incorporates the metaphysical implications of the number 13. The 12 disciples, when combined with the Christ, symbolize the perfected union of individual qualities with divine awareness, forming a wholeness that transcends duality. This sacred number serves as a reminder of our collective purpose to merge the one with the many, bringing forth unity from multiplicity and harmony from diversity.

Let this book be your companion and guide as you embark on this sacred journey—from the son of man to the Sun of God—awakening to the indestructible light within and realizing the profound implications of your divine nature. May it inspire you to rise above the limitations of the lower self, to embrace the higher calling of love, wisdom, and unity, and to walk boldly as a beacon of the eternal Christ within, embodying the profound wisdom and boundless power that is your divine inheritance.

2nd Entry

The Grand Scheme of Evolution and the Cycles of Yugas

In Hindu cosmology, the Yuga cycles represent vast periods of cosmic time, each with its own distinct qualities, energies, and impacts on both the collective and individual spiritual evolution. These cycles—Satya Yuga, Treta Yuga, Dvapara Yuga, and Kali Yuga—progressively embody a descent from a golden age of spiritual unity and wisdom to an age of material entanglement and spiritual decline. Currently, we are in the Kali Yuga, often understood as the darkest and most challenging age, where spiritual and moral degradation reach their peaks, yet it is also a period filled with potential for profound transformation.

Understanding Kali Yuga: The Present Cycle

Kali Yuga, often referred to as the "Age of Darkness," is marked by a significant diminution of dharma, or righteous conduct. During this cycle, humanity experiences an intensified focus on the material world, ego-driven pursuits, and a weakening connection to spiritual principles. On the mental and spiritual planes, Kali Yuga is characterized by the obfuscation of higher truths and an overemphasis on empirical knowledge over inner wisdom. This is the age where the intellect often finds itself restricted to the gross material plane, making it difficult for humanity to perceive subtler realities and the divine essence within.

However, from a metaphysical perspective, Kali Yuga is not just an era of descent. It is also a pivotal stage in the cyclical journey of evolution where the friction of duality—spirit and matter, light and darkness, knowledge and ignorance—serves as a crucible for spiritual growth. It is through the darkness of this age that the Sons of God are tasked with developing discernment, resilience, and a deeper alignment with divine consciousness.

The Role of Conscious Evolution in Kali Yuga

In this period, evolution on the spiritual and mental planes is marked by a unique paradox. While the outer world may seem to fall further into chaos and ignorance, this very environment challenges individuals to awaken inner spiritual faculties. The Kali Yuga serves as a mirror, reflecting the internal struggles of the human psyche and pushing the Sons of God to transcend the limitations imposed by their environment.

On the spiritual plane, this age invites an inward journey. The barriers presented by materialistic tendencies and lower desires act as catalysts for an awakening of the higher self, urging a return to the soul's original purity and unity with the divine. This inner work aligns with the notion that in Kali Yuga, external forms and rituals hold less efficacy, while inner purification and alignment with truth become paramount.

Positioning in the Greater Cycle of Yugas

As we move through the Kali Yuga, it is essential to understand that this phase is both a culmination and a preparation. We are situated in the descending arc of the yugas, where each cycle reveals a further veiling of divine light and truth. However, this descent is also the prelude to an eventual return to higher states in the ascending arc, where spiritual virtues such as Dharma, or righteousness, will once again be reestablished.

In this cosmic cycle, the Kali Yuga represents a period of purification through adversity. The heightened density of this age encourages the shedding of egoic illusions and prepares the ground for a spiritual renewal that will emerge as humanity transitions back into higher yugas. The challenges and turbulence of Kali Yuga are thus opportunities for the Sons of God to accelerate their evolution by cultivating inner qualities that align with higher truths.

Implications for Spiritual and Mental Development

Spiritually, Kali Yuga represents a field where conscious effort is required to awaken and sustain divine insight. The lower nature, often magnified in this age, must be understood, transmuted, and ultimately harmonized with the higher self. The Sons of God, in this era, are called to embody the resilience of truth amidst the dissonance of illusion, transforming their consciousness in preparation for the eventual reawakening of dharma.

On the mental plane, the current cycle demands an evolution from intellectualism to true wisdom. In Kali Yuga, mental faculties are often entangled with materialism and ego-driven pursuits. However, for those who seek higher knowledge, the limitation of intellect in perceiving spiritual truths becomes evident, thereby creating an impulse toward transcendence. Through disciplined introspection, meditation, and the cultivation of divine qualities, the mind can be realigned with the higher spiritual purpose of life.

The Path Forward: Awakening Within the Darkness

The Kali Yuga, while challenging, offers a profound path of initiation for those who embrace it. It is an age that asks the Sons of God to develop a unique strength, rooted in an unshakeable connection to the inner self, unaffected by the flux of the outer world.

By understanding the nature of this cycle, individuals can orient themselves within the larger framework of cosmic evolution, recognizing that each difficulty encountered is an opportunity to rise above, to refine the soul, and to deepen spiritual understanding.

As we collectively journey through Kali Yuga, we find ourselves in a preparatory phase where the deepening of inner awareness becomes the foundation for the spiritual ascent that follows.

For the Sons of God, this period is a call to anchor divine principles within themselves, acting as beacons of light and guiding others toward the remembrance of their own divine heritage.

Through this conscious alignment, the darkness of Kali Yuga transforms into a transformative force, leading to the eventual reestablishment of divine order as humanity progresses toward the higher yugas once more.

3rd Entry

Introduction to the Egyptian Metaphysical Profile Series

In this series of lectures, we delve into the metaphysical profiles of the ancient Egyptian gods and goddesses, approaching them not as mythological figures or distant deities, but as profound embodiments of divine consciousness. These are not merely historical or religious figures; they are metaphysical archetypes, each representing the pinnacle of spiritual development in a particular domain of divine energy. Each god or goddess in the Egyptian pantheon signifies a unique quality of divine consciousness—a perfected state of godliness that illuminates an aspect of the divine mind.

The ancient Egyptians understood these deities as expressions of the universe's multifaceted nature, each one representing a fundamental principle or cosmic law. They believed that these gods embodied the highest state of spiritual refinement and alignment with divine order. When we speak of gods like Thoth, Anubis, or Isis, we are not only exploring their roles in ancient myths but uncovering the profound qualities they represent on a metaphysical level. Each of these figures serves as a mirror to the divine qualities we are called to cultivate within ourselves.

This series aims to present each Egyptian deity as a metaphysical profile—an archetype of a specific divine quality that we, too, can aspire to embody. Thoth, for instance, represents the highest form of wisdom, symbolizing the intellectual and spiritual mastery of divine knowledge. Anubis signifies the transformative journey through shadow and rebirth, guiding the soul through transitions with a pure consciousness. Isis embodies the nurturing, unifying aspect of divine love, the motherly force that sustains life and brings healing.

In studying these gods and goddesses, we are not simply learning about ancient beliefs but inviting these divine qualities into our own consciousness. These deities serve as symbols for energies that exist within each of us, waiting to be awakened and cultivated. By exploring their metaphysical profiles, we begin to see these qualities not as distant ideals but as intrinsic aspects of our own potential. Each god or goddess offers a pathway to understanding and embodying a facet of the divine, ultimately guiding us toward our highest expression of spiritual truth.

The Egyptian metaphysical profiles are part of a larger journey—the process of aligning our minds, hearts, and souls with divine consciousness. By engaging with each archetype, we gain insights into the nature of the divine qualities we are called to develop. These qualities are not random; they are essential to our evolution from ordinary human consciousness toward godliness, a transformation that mirrors the journey of the Sons of Man to the Sons of God.

As we move through this series, we will look deeply into the metaphysical essence of each Egyptian god and goddess, exploring the divine qualities they embody and the lessons they offer for our own spiritual path. This is not merely a study of ancient icons but an invitation to integrate these principles into our lives, awakening our own inner divinity and aligning ourselves with the cosmic order.

Each lecture will reveal the inner structure of these divine archetypes, highlighting the godly qualities they represent and how these qualities can be embodied by us on our spiritual journey. Let this series be a guide as we seek to understand, cultivate, and ultimately live these divine principles, transforming ourselves from seekers into true bearers of divine consciousness.

The Divine Unfolding: A Metaphysical Exploration of Creation

Creation is not a singular act but a continual unfolding of divine potential, reflecting the principles of cosmic order, duality, and self-generation. The archetype of Ra, representing the source of all creation, illustrates the process of divine consciousness manifesting into existence. This journey from formless potential to structured reality offers profound lessons on the nature of existence and the soul's path toward enlightenment.

The Archetype of Khepera: Becoming and Transformation

At the heart of creation lies the principle of becoming, embodied by Khepera, the transformative aspect of divine consciousness. This symbolizes the initial stirring of awareness within the void of unmanifested potential. The act of self-generation emphasizes the inherent power of the divine to bring forth life and order from chaos, reflecting the soul's ability to create through intention and alignment with universal truth.

The Primordial Abyss and the First Duality

Emerging from the infinite waters of Nu, the divine consciousness initiates creation by establishing dualities. Shu and Tefnut, representing air and moisture, embody the forces of separation and cohesion. These dual aspects are the foundation upon which the cosmos is built, demonstrating the interplay of opposites necessary for balance and growth.

- **Nu as Infinite Potential:** The formless abyss is a symbol of latent possibilities, a state of pure potential from which all creation emerges.

- **Shu and Tefnut:** The interplay of these forces mirrors the soul's inner dynamics—expansion and contraction, clarity and nurturing—necessary for spiritual evolution.

The Framework of Space and Time

The separation of Nut (the sky) and Seb (the earth) establishes the structure within which creation unfolds. This act symbolizes the soul's journey through time and space, navigating the interplay of the material and spiritual realms.

- **Nut as the Cosmic Womb:** The celestial dome represents the infinite possibilities of the spiritual plane.

- **Seb as the Foundation:** The grounding force of the material realm provides the platform for divine potential to manifest.

The Multiplication of Life

As creation expands, the archetypal forces of life emerge through Osiris, Isis, Set, and Nephthys. Each represents a fundamental principle in the soul's journey:

- **Osiris:** Renewal and divine kingship, symbolizing spiritual resurrection.

- **Isis:** Intuition and nurturing wisdom, guiding the soul toward higher understanding.

- **Set:** Challenge and disruption, the catalyst for transformation.

- **Nephthys:** Hidden support, the unseen forces that aid the soul's growth.

This multiplication reflects the soul's progression through cycles of growth, decay, and renewal, continually returning to its divine source.

The Eye of Ra: Divine Will and Insight

The Eye of Ra represents the active force of divine will and awareness. Its dual role as both creator and destroyer highlights the necessity of balance in maintaining cosmic harmony. The eye's journey symbolizes the soul's search for truth, which requires the integration of light and shadow.

Tears of Creation

The tears that give birth to life signify the emotional and energetic investment of the divine in creation. This metaphor illustrates that all beings carry the essence of their source, bound together by the principles of Ma'at—truth, harmony, and order.

Rooted in Ma'at

Creation is grounded in the principles of balance and truth. The foundation laid in Ma'at ensures that all manifestations align with divine order. For the soul, this signifies the importance of living in harmony with universal laws to achieve spiritual growth.

The Interplay of Self and Shadow Self

The act of self-creation through reflection and union with the shadow highlights the inherent completeness of the divine. This dynamic interplay illustrates that creation arises from the unity of opposites within the self.

- **Shadow as Potential:** The shadow represents the unmanifest aspects of the soul, waiting to be shaped into form through intention and will.

The Eternal Dance of Dualities

The continual reference to dualities—light and shadow, spirit and matter—underscores their role in maintaining cosmic balance. These opposites are not adversaries but

complementary forces that drive the cycle of creation, preservation, and transformation.

Lessons for the Sons of God

This creation narrative offers profound insights into the metaphysical principles governing existence:

- **Self-Realization:** The divine act of self-generation mirrors the soul's journey to recognize and harness its creative potential.

- **Harmony in Duality:** The interplay of opposites is essential for growth and balance, both in the cosmos and within the soul.

- **Alignment with Truth:** Living in accordance with Ma'at ensures harmony and progression along the spiritual path.

- **Infinite Potential:** The journey from Nu to manifestation reminds the Sons of God of their boundless potential as reflections of the divine.

This metaphysical breakdown reveals that creation is not merely an event but an eternal process of becoming, rooted in divine principles and perpetually guided by the forces of balance and truth. By embodying these lessons, the Sons of God can align themselves with the cosmic order and fulfill their divine purpose.

Nu: *The Primordial Essence of Divine Potential and the Cyclical Path of Enlightenment*

Greetings, Sons of God, seekers on the path of illumination, vessels of the divine essence.

Today, we embark on an exploration that reaches beyond the superficial and into the profound currents of metaphysical understanding. We will delve into the essence of Nu, the primordial goddess, whose significance transcends the confines of time and space, embodying the boundless potential that exists within all creation. Nu is not merely a figure in ancient Egyptian cosmology; she represents the foundational waters of existence, the womb of cosmic possibility, and the source from which all manifestations emerge.

In our study of Nu, we will confront the mystery of potentiality, the power of formlessness, and the spiritual implications of what it means to embody the unmanifest within ourselves. Each of you, as Sons of God, carries within you the potential to reflect the attributes of Nu, to understand her not as an external deity but as an aspect of your own divine nature, the limitless source within.

Nu as the Primordial Waters of Consciousness

Nu is often described as the boundless expanse of waters that existed before creation. In metaphysical terms, she represents the state of undifferentiated consciousness the infinite potential before thought, form, or matter arises. To understand Nu is to peer into the depths of pure being, untainted by attributes or divisions. She is the womb of the universe, the space where all is unified and whole, holding within her the seeds of every possible reality.

Consider this: in her essence, Nu is akin to the silent space of your own higher self, uncolored by the desires, fears, and limitations of the material world. When we tap into this aspect within ourselves, we access a state of unity, where the ego dissolves, and all dualities merge into oneness. This is a place of deep introspection and pure awareness, a reminder that beyond all forms, you are a part of this cosmic ocean of consciousness.

Water as a Metaphor for Divine Truth and Transformation

Nu is symbolized by water—an element that flows, adapts, and nourishes, yet remains unchanged in its essence. Water holds an unparalleled place in metaphysical symbolism, representing purity, unity, and the fluid nature of consciousness. Just as water reflects and adapts, so does divine truth remain pure, embracing all aspects of existence without being tainted by them.

As Sons of God, contemplate the nature of water within you. Your consciousness, like Nu's waters, is capable of assuming many forms—each a temporary expression of an eternal essence. Water cleanses, it moves freely without attachment, and it dissolves barriers, allowing life to flourish. In the same way, aligning with the principle of Nu means learning to embody fluidity in consciousness, letting go of rigid identities, and embracing the boundless nature of spirit. This is a call to purify the self, to remove the barriers of ego, and to flow as the waters of truth.

Nu as the Source of Cosmic Potential and the Cycle of Manifestation

Nu is not only the container of undifferentiated potential but also the wellspring from which all creation emerges. From her depths, Ra arises—the first spark of light that initiates the cycle of manifestation. This is not merely a story of creation; it is an archetype embedded within you. As beings of divine nature, each of you carries within yourself this cycle—the potential to bring forth light from the depths of your inner waters.

This process of manifestation is a journey from the unmanifest to the manifest, from potential to expression. When we meditate on Nu, we see ourselves as the creators of our own reality, drawing forth attributes, ideas, and actions from the silent depths of consciousness. To connect with Nu is to understand the cyclical nature of existence—the emergence from, and eventual return to, the cosmic womb.

Integrating Other Aspects: Nu as the Matrix of All Gods

Nu, in her role as the primal waters, serves as the matrix from which various divine principles emerge. Ra, for example, represents the first light of consciousness that breaks forth from Nu's depths, symbolizing the birth of awareness.

Similarly, the elements of creation, as depicted in other deities like Shu (air) and Tefnut (moisture), all trace their origins to Nu. She is the source from which all archetypes of divinity are born, making her both the mother and the sustainer of the gods.

For you, Sons of God, this holds a profound meaning. It implies that the qualities embodied by each divine archetype—wisdom, power, love, and truth—are all latent within you, awaiting realization. Nu reminds us that our spiritual journey is not about acquiring something external but rather awakening these attributes from within. The gods are not separate entities but symbols of the higher potentials you hold, each one a facet of the limitless essence of Nu that resides in you.

Nu and the Concept of Eternal Recurrence and Renewal

The primordial waters of Nu are timeless. They represent not only the origin but also the return, an eternal cycle of birth, death, and rebirth. Every act of creation, every moment of realization, is a manifestation of Nu's endless cycle of renewal. The universe itself breathes in rhythms—expanding and contracting, manifesting and dissolving—always returning to the womb of Nu, where it finds rest and rejuvenation.

Reflect on this within yourself: your spiritual path is a journey of continuous renewal. Each cycle of growth brings you closer to realizing your divine nature.

In moments of meditation, when you return to the silent, undifferentiated space within, you are reconnecting with the essence of Nu, finding strength and wisdom in the act of letting go. To live in harmony with Nu's principle is to embrace change, to let go of attachments, and to allow each experience to nourish your journey back to the One.

Nu and the Paradox of Formlessness and Form

Nu is the paradox of formlessness giving birth to form, the boundless creating boundaries, the infinite manifesting in the finite. She embodies the supreme principle that the eternal contains within it the potential for the temporal. Every form, every aspect of reality, is a temporary expression of the unmanifest source.

In recognizing Nu's formlessness, we are called to look beyond appearances and recognize the transient nature of the physical world. As Sons of God, you are not merely bodies or personalities but expressions of a higher truth. To embody Nu's wisdom is to live with a sense of detachment from material illusions, understanding that your true essence remains untouched by the ever-changing forms of existence. This is not a denial of life but a deeper engagement with it, knowing that each moment is both a reflection of and a return to the formless divine.

Nu as the Archetype of the Higher Self's Potential

Lastly, Nu's ultimate teaching is the embodiment of limitless potential, a reminder that the highest aspect of your being is a state of pure possibility. Nu calls upon us to return to our own primordial nature, to access the untouched, infinite reservoir of consciousness within. She invites each of us to become creators in our own right, to draw forth wisdom, compassion, and strength from the silent depths of our higher self.

When we connect with Nu, we recognize that the path of enlightenment is not a journey of becoming something new but a return to our original, unbounded nature. The sons of God are called to awaken this potential, to embody the qualities that emerge from the depths of divine consciousness, and to walk as beacons of light, inspiring others on the path of spiritual realization.

In closing, remember that Nu is not an external figure to be worshipped but an archetype to be understood and integrated. She is the silent ocean within each of you, the boundless source from which your highest qualities emerge. Embrace her wisdom, embody her fluidity, and may you each return to the divine waters within, discovering the limitless potential that lies in the depths of your own being.

Shu: *The Breath of Divine Order and Cosmic Harmony*

Today, we delve into the supreme metaphysical embodiment of Shu, not merely as an ancient deity, but as an eternal archetype and force that permeates every aspect of spiritual existence. Shu, the god of air, light, and separation, is a cosmic mediator, a force that upholds the universe's balance and stability. Understanding Shu is understanding the self as a bridge between realms, a harmonizer of forces, and a vessel of divine order.

In contemplating Shu, we will explore his manifestations through various divine archetypes and forces—Nut, Geb, Ra, and Tefnut—revealing Shu as the archetype of divine balance, clarity, and the breath of life itself. Sons of God, I urge you to reflect deeply upon each aspect, recognizing the echoes of Shu within you, for in these qualities lie the keys to your spiritual evolution.

Shu: The Divine Breath and Vital Force

Shu is the very breath of life. When we speak of Shu, we speak of the divine life-force that animates all beings. In ancient texts, Shu is described as the breath or "out-breath" of Ra, the Sun, and through this breath, life is made manifest. This breath is not simply air; it is **prana, chi**, the **vital energy** that sustains us and connects us to the cosmos.

Consider this, Sons of God: each breath you take is a testament to Shu's presence within you. It is a reminder of the divine essence that flows through your very being. Shu's breath is **not passive**; it is an active, dynamic force, filling you with life, animating the body, and allowing the mind to perceive the higher realms. By practicing conscious breathing, you align with Shu, centering yourself in the present, where divine energy flows unimpeded.

Shu: Separator of Heaven and Earth

In ancient mythology, Shu holds Nut, the sky, aloft from Geb, the earth, creating a sacred space where existence unfolds. This act of separation is more than a physical gesture; it is a profound metaphysical act. Shu is the force of discernment, the one who establishes boundaries and creates order in a world otherwise bound to chaos.

Sons of God, what does this mean for you? Shu's act of separating heaven from earth is a call for you to cultivate discernment in your own lives. Just as Shu maintains the boundary between realms, you too must create boundaries that uphold the sanctity of your spirit. This is not separation for the sake of division, but rather separation that enables **clarity and purity**. By holding to your spiritual principles, you create a space within yourself where divine consciousness can thrive.

Shu and Light: The Illumination of Truth

Shu is not only the god of air but also a god of light and clarity. In ancient thought, **light** symbolizes truth, knowledge, and understanding—the qualities that pierce through the veils of ignorance and illusion. Shu brings this light to the world, illuminating what is hidden and casting away shadows.

This light is within you, Sons of God. Shu's light is the illuminating force that resides in the higher mind, guiding you toward understanding and self-realization. In every moment of self-reflection, in every act of wisdom, you are embodying Shu's light. Just as Shu disperses darkness, so too are you called to cultivate clarity, to pursue knowledge, and to act as beacons of light for others on the path of enlightenment.

Shu: The Guardian of Cosmic Order

In his role as the separator, Shu upholds the cosmic order, a principle essential for the harmony of creation. He does not merely separate; he maintains balance and ensures that each aspect of existence has its rightful place. Shu's order is not rigid or oppressive but rather a dynamic stability that sustains the flow of life and spirit.

Sons of God, reflect on how you maintain order within yourselves. Shu's example teaches us that true strength lies in balance. To embody Shu is to hold firm yet be flexible, to establish boundaries yet remain open to divine guidance. Shu's order is a call to cultivate inner stability, to be grounded in your divine essence while adaptable to the changes that life brings. This balance is your foundation, the pillar that enables your higher self to manifest fully.

The Integrative Role of Shu: Harmony Among Forces

In the pantheon, Shu interacts with other deities—Nut, Geb, Ra, and Tefnut—each embodying different forces. Nut, the sky, represents the divine potential, while Geb, the earth, symbolizes manifest creation. Tefnut, Shu's sister, embodies moisture and receptivity, a natural counterpart to Shu's airy nature.

Shu's relationship with Tefnut is a profound symbol of **the balance between active and receptive energies**. In you, Sons of God, this balance reflects the harmony between **doing and being**, between **action and surrender**. Just as Shu and Tefnut work in tandem, you are encouraged to balance your assertive, creative impulses with receptive, intuitive listening. Only in this balance can you find true alignment with the divine.

Shu as the Out-Breath of Divine Will

The mythological role of Shu as Ra's out-breath reflects a cosmic rhythm of **creation and dissolution**, of **expansion and return**. Shu's breath is the pulse of the universe, an eternal cycle that reflects the cycles within our own lives—the cycles of growth, release, and renewal.

Sons of God, contemplate the cyclical nature of Shu's breath. Life is not linear; it moves in waves and cycles. Each breath, each action, each thought, is part of this cosmic rhythm. To align with Shu is to recognize the ebb and flow within yourself, to understand that there is a time for action and a time for stillness. Just as Shu breathes forth creation, so too must you breathe forth your intentions, allowing them to manifest and eventually return to source.

Shu and the Power of Boundaries

Shu's act of holding Nut and Geb apart is an affirmation of the necessity of boundaries—not only in the physical but also in the metaphysical sense. Boundaries are the structures that protect your spiritual integrity, the sacred spaces that allow divine energy to flow without contamination.

In your journey, **Sons of God**, Shu calls you to discern where you need boundaries and where you may need to let go. As he held the heavens aloft, you too must rise to hold your higher self in sacred separation from the distractions and illusions of the lower world. This does not imply rejection of the material; rather, it is an invitation to hold space for the divine within you.

Shu: Embodying the Divine Spark Within

To fully understand Shu is to see him as a reflection of the divine spark within. Shu is the outpouring of divine will, the breath of life, the force of light, and the guardian of cosmic order. To embody Shu is to embody these principles in your own life.

When you act with discernment, when you breathe consciously, when you balance the forces of light and dark within you, you are not merely imitating Shu—you are manifesting the essence of Shu within yourself. Each moment of clarity, each act of order, each breath filled with intention is a testament to Shu's presence in you.

Conclusion: Shu as the Eternal Archetype of Divine Harmony

Sons of God, Shu is not just a deity of ancient myth; he is an archetype of divine harmony that calls each of you to recognize your place in the cosmos. To walk in the path of Shu is to live with clarity, balance, and integrity, to be the bridge between heaven and earth, and to hold the divine light within you as a beacon for others.

Let Shu's qualities guide you as you navigate the realms of existence. In every breath, feel the presence of divine life-force. In every boundary you set, recognize the sacred space it creates. In every act of balance, know that you are aligning with the cosmic order, embodying the eternal archetype of Shu.

In this way, Shu is not separate from you; he is the force within you that sustains, clarifies, and harmonizes. As you embody Shu, may you become pillars of divine light and truth, holding space for the eternal as you journey ever closer to enlightenment.

Hetep: *The Divine Manifestation of Equilibrium and the Spiritual Union of All Selves*

Greetings, Sons of God. Today, we explore the profound metaphysical dimensions embodied in Hetep, an ancient and sacred symbol of the Divine Will, an unspoken Word, and the equilibrium that transcends all dualities. Hetep represents the silence of divine expression, hidden in its essence yet manifesting through the principles of balance, peace, and ultimate unity. As we journey through this profile, we shall uncover the layered attributes of Hetep, understanding not only its symbolic resonance but also its implications on our own path toward spiritual harmony.

The Divine Will and Logos

Hetep is not merely a deity but a metaphysical embodiment of the Divine Will, or Logos—the silent yet potent energy that permeates all levels of existence. This Divine Will is hidden, an unuttered Word that echoes through the stillness, manifesting only in those who have ascended beyond the superficial layers of ego. Hetep is the quiet force of balance, a presence felt but seldom perceived, symbolizing the ultimate state of equilibrium that we, as Sons of God, must aspire to attain.

The essence of Hetep reminds us that true power lies not in overt actions but in silent purpose. The Divine Will, as embodied by Hetep, calls us to embrace this stillness, allowing our own inner voice to resonate with the higher frequencies of the Universe. The Word, when finally uttered, becomes a manifestation of divine truth, guiding the soul beyond the realms of material form and into the essence of pure consciousness. The Secret Utterance and the Emanation of Life

The life force that emanates from Hetep is a sacred, unseen current that flows through all creation, guiding the soul in its journey from inception to transcendence. This energy is beyond the cycles of birth and death, existing within a plane of pure essence that only the enlightened ego can perceive. Hetep, as a symbol of this secret utterance, invites us to recognize the interconnectedness of all forms within the Divine Life, expressed as a harmonious whole.

In the silence of Hetep's hidden utterance, we come to understand the cyclical nature of existence, represented by the *manvantara*, or cycles of creation and dissolution. These cycles reflect the ebb and flow of divine energy, a rhythm that is not bound by time but by the consciousness that perceives it. The Sons of God must align themselves with this rhythm, finding within it the eternal dance of creation and the return to oneness.

The Love of God and the Equilibrium of the Soul

Hetep embodies the Love of God—not as an emotional attachment but as an intuitive understanding that all things within the cosmic order serve a purpose for the greater good. This divine love is an awareness that transcends the boundaries of individuality, recognizing the interconnectedness of all life. To know and love God, as Hetep teaches, is to accept the inherent goodness and justice that pervades the Universe, even amidst apparent chaos.

This divine love is a transformative force, drawing us toward a state of equilibrium within the soul. Hetep symbolizes this balance, an inner peace that arises when we perceive all dualities as necessary expressions of the Divine. In this way, Hetep guides us to a higher plane of existence, where we are no longer subject to the fluctuations of desire and aversion but remain centered in the unity of being.

The Pillars of Shu and the Four Planes of Manifestation

The symbolism of Hetep is intimately connected with the *Pillars of Shu*, representing the four planes of manifestation that exist beneath the atma, or Divine Self. These pillars are the structural elements of the Universe, separating time and space and establishing the foundational layers of existence. Each plane represents a different aspect of divine expression, from the physical to the metaphysical, all held in balance by the divine will of Shu, with Hetep as its silent overseer.

In Hetep's presence, these planes unify, dissolving into one another as we transcend beyond the material world. It is through understanding the function of each plane that we begin to see the totality of our own existence—physical, emotional, mental, and spiritual—all harmonized under the guidance of Hetep. This integration brings about a state of divine equilibrium, a reflection of the balance inherent in the cosmic order.

The Mouth as the Instrument of Divine Speech

Hetep, often referred to as the silent God, reminds us of the sacredness of speech and the power of unspoken words. The mouth, as a symbol for Hetep, is not merely an organ of verbal expression but a gateway for divine truths. In silence, the mouth of Hetep reveals truths beyond the intellect, connecting the soul with the higher realms of divine understanding. This silent speech represents the expression of latent potential, the bridge between thought and manifestation.

As Sons of God, we are called to cultivate this silent power within us, learning to perceive without words, to communicate with the Universe in ways that transcend spoken language. The mouth of Hetep is an emblem of this inner strength, a reminder that true wisdom is often found not in what is said but in what is understood within.

The Sword of the Spirit and the Dispelling of Ignorance

In Hetep's hand is the Sword of the Spirit, a symbol of divine intuition that cuts through ignorance and illusion. This sword represents the clarity that arises from spiritual insight, the ability to see beyond the veils of maya and perceive the truth within. Hetep's sword is not wielded in violence but as a beacon of enlightenment, guiding the soul toward self-realization.

The Sword of the Spirit aligns with Hetep's role as a dispeller of falsehoods. It is a tool for the Sons of God, a means of discerning the real from the unreal, of navigating the spiritual path with precision and clarity. As we hold this sword within ourselves, we invoke the strength to overcome the lower self and ascend into higher realms of consciousness, where truth shines unobstructed.

Hetep, the Lake of Divine Union

Finally, Hetep is the Lake, a symbol of the Greater Self where all lesser selves unite as one. In this lake, the fragmented aspects of the individual merge into a single, undivided consciousness. It is a space of purity and reflection, where the waters of divine wisdom cleanse the soul and reveal the true nature of being. The lake of Hetep calls us to recognize the oneness that underlies all multiplicity, inviting us to immerse ourselves in the collective essence of divinity.

This union in Hetep's lake symbolizes the atma-buddhi, the higher planes of existence where individual egos dissolve into the Greater Self. For the Sons of God, this lake represents the culmination of the spiritual journey, the return to source where all distinctions vanish, and we are left with only the pure, undivided spirit.

Conclusion: Returning to Hetep Within

As we conclude this exploration of Hetep, let us remember that Hetep is not an external deity but an inner state of equilibrium and divine will. It is the silent force within us, guiding us toward the realization of our true selves. Hetep teaches us that peace is not found in the absence of conflict but in the acceptance of all things as expressions of the Divine.

In embodying Hetep, we become vessels of divine balance, channels of unspoken wisdom, and beacons of spiritual clarity. May each of us, as Sons of God, cultivate this sacred silence within, allowing the divine equilibrium of Hetep to permeate every aspect of our being, guiding us toward the ultimate unity of all things.

Reflection Exercise for the Sons of God

1. Reflect on the aspects of your own life that are out of balance. How can the principles of Hetep guide you toward restoring equilibrium within?

2. Practice silent meditation, focusing on the unuttered Word within. Observe how stillness itself can become a source of profound wisdom.
3. Contemplate the Sword of the Spirit within you, asking yourself what illusions or false beliefs you need to release to embrace a clearer understanding of truth.

In the spirit of Hetep, may we walk forth in peace, embodying the silent strength and eternal balance that are our divine heritage.

Ma'at: *The Cosmic Scale of Truth - Unveiling the Metaphysics*

Greetings, Sons of God. Today we turn to one of the most profound principles in metaphysics: Ma'at. She is not merely a goddess of ancient Egypt but the living essence of cosmic law, truth, and divine harmony. Ma'at is the framework upon which all existence rests, the scale by which all actions are measured, and the eternal order that binds the seen and unseen realms into coherence. She is the invisible architect of balance, ensuring that the higher realms of spirit and the lower planes of matter remain interconnected and interdependent.

Ma'at is the embodiment of the Law of Karma, the force that harmonizes every action, thought, and intention with the greater cosmic equilibrium. Her feather, so light it measures only the purity of the heart, is the ultimate symbol of alignment with divine truth. Yet, Ma'at is not limited to justice or retribution; she is the vibration of truth itself—the eternal rhythm that guides the soul's journey through the dimensions of physical, emotional, mental, causal, and spiritual planes. In essence, Ma'at teaches us that every breath, every decision, and every interaction is an opportunity to harmonize with the divine. Her justice is not punitive but evolutionary, calling the Sons of God to rise above the illusions of ego and duality and live as vessels of truth, light, and eternal balance.

To understand Ma'at is to recognize the interconnectedness of all things. Her presence is the thread that weaves the cosmos into unity, ensuring that no soul, no action, and no intention is ever lost to chaos. In embodying Ma'at, the Sons of God become architects of divine order, reflections of her eternal principles, and participants in the sacred dance of creation. This is the path to enlightenment—to live in harmony with the laws of Ma'at is to align with the highest truth of the universe itself.

Ma'at: The Eternal Principle of Divine Balance

Sons of God, we approach the profound and multidimensional principle of Ma'at, the cosmic force that transcends mere mythology and permeates the very fabric of existence. Ma'at is the cornerstone of metaphysical order, the divine mechanism through which the higher and lower realms are maintained in harmony. She governs not only the external universe but also the intricate workings of the soul. Today, we shall explore her attributes, her profound relationships with Ra and Thoth, her place in ancient texts, and the metaphysical implications of her immutable laws.

Ma'at: The Daughter of Ra and the Cosmic Order

As the daughter of Ra, Ma'at emanates from the Supreme Self, embodying the manifestation of divine will and universal law. Ra, as the Logos, represents the source of creation—the eternal light from which all emerges. Ma'at is born of this light, signifying that the principles of truth and balance are intrinsic to the very act of creation. Her existence ensures that the cosmos operates not in chaos but in a state of unchanging regularity and order.

This relationship reveals that Ma'at is not a subordinate entity but an extension of Ra's divine essence. She is the active force that sustains the duality of heaven and earth, ensuring that opposites such as light and darkness, spirit and matter, remain in equilibrium. To the Sons of God, this teaches that divine law is inherent in every aspect of existence, and by aligning with Ma'at, one aligns with the eternal will of the Supreme Self.

Ma'at: The Wife of Thoth and the Union of Truth and Wisdom

The marriage of Ma'at to Thoth symbolizes the sacred union of truth and wisdom. Thoth, the divine mind, bridges the higher and lower planes, functioning as the intermediary that translates cosmic truth into comprehensible form. As the embodiment of wisdom, Thoth provides the structure through which Ma'at's principles are enacted. This union signifies that truth (Ma'at) cannot exist without the discernment and expression of wisdom (Thoth), and wisdom loses its purpose without the grounding of truth.

In this sacred partnership, Ma'at provides the foundation of cosmic law, while Thoth ensures its expression in the mental and spiritual planes. For the Sons of God, this signifies that their higher mind (Thoth) must align with their soul's truth (Ma'at) to act as vessels of divine order.

This union also underscores the necessity of living a balanced life, where intellect serves the higher purpose of aligning with eternal truth.

The Feather of Ma'at: A Symbol of Lightness and Purity

Ma'at's feather, used in the weighing of the heart, is a profound symbol of spiritual alignment. The feather signifies the lightness of the soul that has transcended ego, illusion, and attachment. In the Judgment Hall of Osiris, the heart of the deceased is weighed against this feather, determining whether the soul has lived in accordance with divine law. This act is not punitive but transformative, offering the soul an opportunity to realign with Ma'at's principles.

The feather's lightness also represents the transient nature of the lower personality, which must give way to the eternal truth of the Higher Self. Sons of God are called to embody this feather-like quality, living with integrity, humility, and alignment with cosmic truth. To live in Ma'at is to release the weight of falsehood and embrace the purity of divine order.

Karma and the Law of Ma'at

Ma'at is the metaphysical embodiment of karma, the immutable law of cause and effect. Her presence ensures that every action, thought, and intention is harmonized with the greater cosmic balance. Karma, under Ma'at's guidance, is not a system of punishment but a mechanism of spiritual evolution, aligning the lower self with the Higher Self through cycles of experience.

Metaphysically, this reveals that Ma'at operates as the great harmonizer, weaving the soul's journey through the dimensions of physical, emotional, mental, causal, and spiritual planes. Each plane reflects an aspect of Ma'at's law, teaching the soul to integrate lessons and rise to higher states of consciousness. Sons of God must recognize that every choice they make is weighed in Ma'at's balance, shaping their journey toward divine alignment.

Ma'at and the Governance of the Gods

In ancient Egyptian texts, it is said that even the gods live by Ma'at's principles. This profound statement underscores that Ma'at's laws are not merely human constructs but universal truths that govern all levels of existence. From Ra to Osiris, from Isis to Anubis, all divine archetypes operate under her immutable law.

This reveals the supreme significance of Ma'at as the sustaining force of the cosmos. Her presence in prayers, invocations, and sacred rituals ensures that every act is aligned with divine order. To the Sons of God, this signifies that living by Ma'at is not merely a moral imperative but a cosmic necessity, for it aligns one's will with the eternal rhythm of the universe.

Ma'at in the Judgment Hall: The Soul's Alignment with Truth

The Judgment Hall of Osiris, where the heart is weighed against the feather of Ma'at, symbolizes the soul's ultimate test of alignment. Here, Thoth records the soul's journey, while Anubis, representing the physical body, guides the scales. The heart, representing the causal body or Divine Hall, carries the weight of the soul's experiences, while the feather measures its alignment with truth.

This scene is a powerful metaphor for self-realization. The Sons of God are reminded that every aspect of their being—physical, emotional, mental, and spiritual—must align with Ma'at to achieve liberation. The judgment is not external but internal, calling each soul to examine its own actions, intentions, and alignment with the divine.

The Eternal Presence of Ma'at in Mythology

Ma'at's presence is ubiquitous in ancient Egyptian mythology, appearing in prayers, rituals, and sacred texts. She is invoked in the opening of the mouth ceremony, the recitation of the 42 Negative Confessions, and the invocation of divine protection.

Her consistent presence signifies that no act, no thought, and no ritual is complete without alignment with her principles.

This teaches the Sons of God that Ma'at is not a distant concept but a living presence that permeates every aspect of existence. To honor Ma'at is to honor the divine order within oneself and the universe. Her principles are the keys to enlightenment, offering a path to transcendence and unity with the Absolute.

Conclusion: The Path of Ma'at

Sons of God, to understand Ma'at is to understand the very essence of existence. She is the balance that sustains the cosmos, the truth that guides the soul, and the law that harmonizes all realms. Her presence calls you to live as reflections of divine order, aligning every thought, word, and action with her eternal principles. By embodying Ma'at, you become co-creators of cosmic harmony, participants in the sacred dance of creation, and beacons of light along the path to enlightenment.

Thoth: *The Divine Architect of Knowledge - The Divine Scribe and Mind of Creation*

Sons of God, today we delve into the mysteries of a profound being, one who stands as a bridge between intellect and spirit, embodying both the logic of creation and the intuitive flow of wisdom. Thoth, god of wisdom, writing, and divine knowledge, is an archetype not only within Egyptian cosmology but also within the very structure of our consciousness. As we consider Thoth, we must recognize that his attributes mirror our inner potential, guiding us toward self-realization.

The **Papyrus Boat of Isis** serves as a powerful symbol here. Just as Thoth is the keeper of records, the papyrus represents the journey of divine knowledge that traverses realms, symbolizing Thoth's role as the ferryman of wisdom, moving seamlessly between worlds.

Thoth as the Divine Scribe and Keeper of Sacred Knowledge

Thoth is not only the cosmic scribe but also the keeper of sacred knowledge, embodying the Logos, or divine word, the vibrational blueprint that shapes reality itself. As the **divine scribe**, Thoth encapsulates the essence of existence, where every word, symbol, and glyph associated with him carries a profound energetic resonance. For us, Sons of God, understanding Thoth's role means recognizing that every thought and action we take becomes part of the cosmic record. Thoth shows us that sacred knowledge is not static but a living force evolving within each of us.

In this role, Thoth parallels the **Ark of the Testimony**, which symbolizes the soul's "causal body"—the inner receptacle where divine presence is both revered and realized. Just as Moses placed the tablets within the Ark, we place our thoughts and deeds into the sacred space of our consciousness, each moment evidencing our spiritual evolution or stagnation.

The Cosmic Scribe and Keeper of Divine Records

Thoth, as the cosmic scribe, meticulously records all events in the book of life, capturing each thought, action, and intention with absolute clarity. This act of witnessing calls us, Sons of God, to cultivate a mindful presence within ourselves, to become scribes of our own minds, observing our inner dialogues and actions without attachment. Just as Thoth maintains cosmic order through his record-keeping, so too must we keep careful watch over our thoughts, inscribing each moment on the scroll of our consciousness with awareness.

In this practice of mindful observation, we connect with what ancient texts refer to as *Mahat*, the higher intellect and the plane of creation. Thoth's wisdom guides us here, showing that true knowledge is not the mere accumulation of facts but an evolving understanding rooted in divine perception.

His role as the cosmic scribe parallels the cosmic Ark, reminding us that divine knowledge requires purity and humility in interpretation. When we hold this space for witnessing, we align with the infallibility of divine inspiration, allowing us to discern truth from illusion.

In following Thoth's example, we elevate the soul to a higher plane, where every experience becomes a lesson, every lesson a step toward self-mastery. Our task, then, is to seek and honor this inner scribe, aligning ourselves with the wisdom that leads to self-realization and cosmic harmony.

Thoth, Hermes, and Hermes Trismegistus – The Triune Wisdom

The connection between Thoth and his aspect as **Hermes Trismegistus**, or the "Thrice-Great," reveals the layers of wisdom that Thoth embodies across different dimensions. This triune wisdom operates through the material, intellectual, and spiritual realms, bringing them into divine harmony. Sons of God, as we understand this layered wisdom, we are reminded to seek knowledge on multiple levels—intellectually, to grasp it with our minds; spiritually, to embody it within our souls; and energetically, to express it as a living truth. In doing so, we transcend dualistic thought and move toward a state of divine unity.

Thoth, as the cosmic principle, embodies this triadic structure, calling us to harmonize these three realms within ourselves. The wisdom we seek should therefore permeate not only our minds but resonate within our spirit, guiding us to a holistic understanding of existence.

Thoth and the Art of Intuition and Intellect

Thoth stands at the intersection of intellect and intuition, symbolized by the integration of **Buddhi** (intuition) and **Manas** (intellect). Thoth teaches us that while intellect is essential for organization and categorization, it must be aligned with the higher order of intuitive insight. Just as the **cherubim** guard the garden of Eden, our intellect must act as a gatekeeper, protecting our spiritual journey by discerning truth with clarity.

In this role, Thoth harmonizes the rational with the intuitive, calling us to elevate our understanding from mere knowledge to wisdom. This balance, which transcends form and allows us to perceive spiritual truths, is an invitation to align the mind with the heart, purifying the intellect through compassion and insight.

The Caduceus and the Serpents – Symbols of Healing and Duality

The **caduceus**, often associated with Hermes, holds deep metaphysical significance when tied to Thoth. This symbol of two serpents entwined around a central rod represents dual forces—light and dark, masculine and feminine, passive and active.

Within Thoth's wisdom, the caduceus becomes more than a symbol of physical healing; it represents alchemical transformation, where dualities merge in harmony. For the Sons of God, the serpents signify the rising of **kundalini** energy along the spine, which, when harmonized, illuminates the soul. Thoth teaches that healing occurs when we embrace and balance these polarities within, achieving a synthesis that mirrors the cosmic order.

Thoth's Hammer: The Power of Transformation

In Norse mythology, Thor's **Mjölnir** represents the mind's transformative power; Thoth, too, wields this hammer of divine intellect. Here, Thoth aligns with the **Shekinah**, the indwelling glory within, as a force of transformation that purifies and elevates. The Shekinah, like Thoth's wisdom, calls upon us to align our lower desires with divine will, allowing our mind to become an instrument for conscious creation.

Just as Thoth's hammer transforms the mundane into the divine, so too must we transform our thoughts and intentions. Thoth's wisdom is a reminder that true power arises from inner mastery, demanding rigorous self-discipline and alignment with higher principles.

Geometry and the Divine Blueprint of Creation

Thoth is the architect of **sacred geometry**, the divine language that constructs the universe. From the triangle to the circle, each geometric shape embodies a cosmic principle, vibrating with purpose. The Sons of God are invited to see these forms as representations of spiritual truths, where the **triangle** symbolizes the unity of body, mind, and spirit, and the **circle** represents eternity and unity.

Thoth's sacred geometry reflects the universe's intentional structure, calling upon us to recognize and honor the divine blueprint both within ourselves and in the world around us.

Thoth as the Symbol of Self-Knowledge and Liberation

Thoth, as the guide through the underworld, assists the soul in transcending its attachments and egoic binds, acting as a beacon of liberation that illuminates the journey toward self-awareness. This journey echoes the Papyrus Boat of Isis, which ferries the seeker through realms of shadow, bearing fragments of divine wisdom that ultimately restore wholeness. Thoth's liberation is not about escaping suffering but about transforming it, leading us to confront and conquer our inner Set, the god of chaos, who represents the forces of illusion and separation from our higher selves.

In the Egyptian tradition, Thoth is depicted with the power to "loose the bandages of Set which fetter my mouth," symbolizing his role in liberating the soul from lower desires and illusions. This liberation is not an external act but an inner transformation, where we unbind ourselves from limiting beliefs, fears, and ego-driven desires. Thoth's presence serves as the inner Shekinah, the indwelling divine light, leading us from the chains of ego to the freedom of self-realization. To embody Thoth is to embrace this path of self-liberation, understanding that true freedom emerges from within as we dismantle illusions and reclaim our divine origin. Thoth calls us to see ourselves beyond material desires, to recognize that our essence lies in unity with the divine, not in attachment to the transient.

Thoth and the Moon – The Power of Reflection

Thoth's association with the **moon** underscores his role as a reflective deity, illuminating the hidden recesses of the soul. Just as the moon reflects the sun, Thoth reflects divine wisdom into our minds, encouraging introspection and the uncovering of subconscious truths. The lunar influence of Thoth guides us to look within and recognize the mysteries that lie in silence and solitude.

For the Sons of God, Thoth's lunar symbolism is a reminder that enlightenment is not solely about outward knowledge but an inner journey of self-reflection and transformation.

The Word Made Manifest: Thoth and the Power of Creation

Thoth represents the Word, the divine Logos, through which all creation unfolds. As the *sons of God*, we, too, wield the power of the Word, whether through our speech, thoughts, or intentions. Words are not mere sounds or symbols; they are vehicles of creation. In alignment with Thoth's essence, let our words and thoughts reflect our highest truths, spoken with intention and purpose, shaping a world that mirrors the divine within us.

To speak as Thoth does is to understand the sacredness of words, recognizing that they carry the potential to uplift, inspire, and transform. Let every word we utter be a reflection of divine will, a bridge between the seen and the unseen, the temporal and the eternal.

Thoth's Role in the Underworld and the Weighing of the Heart

As the guide of souls, Thoth presides over the **weighing of the heart** in the underworld, where it is measured against the feather of **Ma'at**—truth, balance, and justice. This ritual is more than a judgment; it is a reflection of cosmic balance. For the Sons of God, the weighing of the heart serves as a reminder that enlightenment requires purity, integrity, and alignment with divine principles.

To walk with Thoth is to commit to living in harmony with Ma'at, understanding that our actions are weighed on the scales of cosmic order.

Thoth's Sacred Animal – The Ibis as a Symbol of Precision

The **ibis**, Thoth's sacred animal, symbolizes focus, precision, and alignment with higher wisdom. Its deliberate movements remind us that spiritual knowledge demands attention to detail and dedication. Just as the ibis treads carefully, so too must we approach spiritual pursuits with discipline and clarity.

Thoth's wisdom calls us to cultivate this precision in our own spiritual practices, demonstrating that true understanding requires commitment and intention.

Thoth's Staff – The Rod of Power and Transformation

Thoth's **staff**, entwined with serpents, symbolizes authority over earthly and spiritual realms. This rod embodies the power of transformation, highlighting the alchemical process of uniting opposites. For the Sons of God, Thoth's staff is a call to harness our spiritual potential, rising above base desires and awakening to divine energy within.

Introduction to the Eighth and Ninth Discourse

As we explore the metaphysical profile of Thoth, the archetype of divine wisdom and the higher mind, it is fitting to consider the Hermetic discourse on the Eighth and Ninth Realms. This profound teaching reveals the soul's ascension through layers of consciousness, guided by the principles of divine order and spiritual insight. In the context of Thoth's role as a bridge between the human and divine, the discourse offers a glimpse into the transformative journey of the soul as it moves from the limitations of material perception to the expansive truth of unity with the Divine Mind. Let us now delve into this mystical journey and uncover its metaphysical significance.

The Eighth and Ninth: A Metaphysical Journey

The **Eighth Realm** symbolizes the stage of spiritual awakening where the soul transcends the limitations of material consciousness. It is a realm of purification, where dualities dissolve, and the higher faculties of the soul—intuition, imagination, and divine intellect—become activated. The **Ninth Realm**, by contrast, represents the ultimate union with the Divine Mind, the realm of universal oneness and truth. Together, these realms encapsulate the path of the Son of God, as a metaphysical archetype, ascending to divine perfection.

The Role of Thoth as a Guide

Thoth, as the divine scribe and keeper of cosmic wisdom, mirrors the role of Hermes Trismegistus in the discourse. Just as Hermes initiates his son into higher realms, Thoth represents the guiding force within us—the higher intellect (buddhi-manas) that bridges the human and divine. Thoth's association with wisdom and the recording of divine truth signifies the process of inscribing spiritual understanding onto the soul, akin to carving the sacred teachings onto "steles of turquoise".

Thoth's wisdom teaches us that spiritual ascent is a step-by-step process, as emphasized in the discourse: "If you hold in mind each one of the steps." The stages of this ascent align with the zodiac's cyclical journey, where each sign offers lessons that prepare the soul for higher states of awareness.

The Symbolism of the Eighth Realm: The Zodiac and Cosmic Order

In the zodiacal framework, the **Eighth Realm** resonates with the energy of **Scorpio**, the sign of transformation, depth, and rebirth. Scorpio represents the alchemical process of shedding lower attachments to reveal the soul's true nature.

As the soul journeys through Scorpio's influence, it learns to master the hidden forces within, preparing for the spiritual illumination of the Ninth Realm.

The process described in the discourse, where Hermes speaks of conceiving and giving birth to the power within, reflects Scorpio's role in spiritual alchemy. This "birth" is the emergence of the higher self, symbolized by the activation of the pineal gland or third eye—a faculty often associated with divine insight and intuition.

The Ninth Realm: Unity and the Divine Mind

The Ninth Realm corresponds to the archetype of **Pisces**, the final stage of the zodiacal cycle. Pisces symbolizes the dissolution of the ego and the merging of the individual soul with the universal consciousness. In the discourse, this is the state where the son declares, "I see the one that moves me from pure forgetfulness." This moment represents the soul's awakening to its divine origin and purpose.

The silent hymn sung in the Ninth Realm, described as "a hymn in silence," signifies the ineffable nature of divine truth.

In metaphysics, this is the point where language and thought are transcended, and the soul communicates directly with the divine through vibration and frequency, as symbolized by the sacred syllables and sounds in the text.

The Father-Son Relationship: A Metaphysical Perspective

The relationship between Hermes and his son reflects the eternal connection between the human soul and the divine source. Metaphysically, Hermes represents the higher self or divine mind, while the son symbolizes the evolving soul seeking to return to its origin. The dialogue between them mirrors the inner dialogue within each of us—the interplay between the spiritual aspiration of the soul and the guiding wisdom of the higher self.

This relationship also resonates with the zodiacal archetypes of **Cancer** and **Capricorn**, representing the soul's nurturing and aspirational qualities. Cancer (the mother) nurtures the soul's growth, while Capricorn (the father) guides it toward spiritual mastery.

The Importance of Silence and Vibration

The emphasis on silent hymns and sacred sounds in the discourse aligns with the teachings of Thoth, who governs the Word (Logos) and its creative power. Silence, in this context, is not the absence of sound but a state of receptive stillness where divine frequencies can be perceived. The sacred syllables—"A O EE O EEE"—represent the vibrational essence of creation, akin to the "Om" of Eastern traditions.

These vibrations activate the higher chakras, aligning the soul with the divine will.

The Eighth and Ninth as Archetypal Realms

The Eighth and Ninth Realms can also be understood through the lens of Egyptian mythology:

The **Eighth Realm** represents the domain of **Nephthys**, the goddess of hidden wisdom and transformation. Nephthys guides the soul through the shadowed aspects of consciousness, preparing it for the illumination of the Ninth Realm.

The **Ninth Realm** aligns with **Ra**, the solar deity embodying ultimate enlightenment and unity. Ra's light reveals the divine order and the soul's place within it, culminating in the realization of universal truth.

The Journey Through the Realms

The son's progression through the realms parallels the journey of the zodiac, where each stage represents a lesson in spiritual growth. The father's instruction to "remember the progress that came to you as wisdom in the books" highlights the importance of integrating these lessons. Just as the zodiac's cycles guide the soul through stages of development, the discourse emphasizes that each step is essential for reaching the ultimate goal of divine union.

The Spiritual Sacrifice: Entering the Ninth

The sacrificial aspect of the journey, where the son offers spiritual sacrifices "with all our heart and our soul and all our strength," echoes the transformative process of **Virgo**. This sign represents the purification of the self, a necessary step before entering the Ninth Realm of oneness and completion.

The Eighth and Ninth as the Pinnacle of the Soul's Journey

The **Discourse on the Eighth and Ninth** encapsulates the essence of the metaphysical journey—moving from separation to unity, from ignorance to divine wisdom. By integrating the teachings of Thoth, the zodiac, and Egyptian mythology, we see that this journey is universal, reflecting the path of every soul toward self-realization.

The eighth and ninth discourse reminds us that the "Sun of God" is not merely an individual but a principle within each of us, guiding us through the stages of growth and enlightenment. Whether through the transformative power of Scorpio, the compassionate surrender of Pisces, or the guiding wisdom of Thoth, the journey to the Eighth and Ninth Realms is a testament to the eternal quest for divine truth and unity.

Conclusion: The Path of Thoth as a Blueprint for Enlightenment

Suns of God, Thoth offers more than knowledge; he offers a pathway to self-realization. His wisdom teaches that enlightenment is a continuous journey of inner transformation. Through Thoth, we understand that the universe is an interconnected web of intelligence, and each of us plays a role in its unfolding.

To embody Thoth is to commit to a life of balance, introspection, and truth. Recognize that every thought, word, and action resonates throughout the cosmos, shaping existence. Let this path of Thoth not only inform you but transform you, guiding you to become bearers of light and wisdom in the journey toward enlightenment.

Imhotep: *Divine Healer and Manifestation of the Higher Self*

Greetings, Suns of God. Today, we embark on a profound journey into the metaphysical essence of Imhotep, a symbol not merely of healing but of the Higher Self manifesting through the mental plane. Imhotep, revered by the ancients as a physician, architect, and priest, serves as a bridge between the physical and divine realms. His name, meaning "he who comes in peace," is a declaration of harmony and healing that transcends mere bodily ailments, reaching into the spiritual and mental realms where true healing occurs.

Imhotep, in his essence, is an archetype of the Higher Self—the perfected self that embodies wisdom, love, and divine intelligence. His role in ancient Egyptian thought was not simply that of a healer but of one who could harmonize the soul and elevate it through wisdom, a quality seen in the archetypal "Physician" as a divine bringer of harmony. To understand Imhotep's role, we must explore his symbolic connections to alchemy, the mental plane, magic, and the serpent—a potent emblem of transformation and divine wisdom.

Alchemy and the Inner Transmutation of the Soul

Imhotep's healing power is not limited to the physical but extends to alchemical transformation, where the base qualities of the lower self are transmuted into the refined essence of the higher. Alchemy, as we understand it metaphysically, is the unperceived process through which the lower nature—the base metal of the soul—is transfigured into spiritual gold. Imhotep, as a divine alchemist, guides the soul through this process, using the fire of divine wisdom to purify and elevate.

In the metaphysical process of alchemy, the three principles—Blackness, Whiteness, and Redness—represent stages of the soul's journey from impurity to divine illumination. This journey aligns with the Egyptian understanding of death and rebirth, where the "black earth" of ignorance is transmuted into the "gold of wisdom." Imhotep's role as a healer encompasses this process of spiritual refinement, for he helps the soul release its lower attachments and emerge as pure spirit.

The Mental Plane: The Central Stage of Divine Manifestation

Imhotep's influence extends into the mental plane, the realm where divine ideas take form. This plane is a bridge between the spiritual and the physical, where thought-forms and divine archetypes are projected into the material world. The mental plane is a vast and dynamic field, one where the Higher Self shapes the lower self through the crystallization of divine ideas.

Imhotep embodies this principle as the "Scribe of the Gods," recording divine wisdom onto the soul in a way that the lower mind can comprehend. Here, thought is the vessel for divine truth, and Imhotep's role is to channel this wisdom, guiding the soul to understand and manifest it within the bounds of physical existence. As we attune ourselves to the mental plane, we connect with Imhotep's archetype, allowing us to transform our thoughts into a divine reflection of our Higher Self.

Magic and the Power of the Higher Mind

Imhotep's association with magic in the ancient texts refers to the inner workings of the Higher Mind, which operates through the subtle realms to achieve transformation. Magic, in this sense, is not the manipulation of the external world but

the inner realization of divine truth. It is through this divine magic that Imhotep performs the "miracles" attributed to him—healing the sick, reviving the dead, and harmonizing the soul with divine will.

This magic aligns with the power of Buddhi, the spiritual wisdom of the Higher Self that uplifts and redeems the soul. Imhotep, in his capacity as the divine physician, harnesses this wisdom to heal on all levels, transmuting the soul's impurities and aligning it with the cosmic order. His magic is a reflection of divine love and wisdom, qualities that each Sun of God must cultivate within to awaken their own divine potential.

The Serpent: Symbol of Wisdom and Duality

The serpent, often associated with Imhotep's healing powers, represents the dual forces of the higher and lower natures within the soul. The higher serpent is atma-buddhic, symbolizing divine wisdom, while the lower serpent is kama-manasic, representing the desire-nature. These forces are inherently opposed yet interdependent, acting as the dynamic tension through which the soul evolves.

Imhotep, as the master of the serpent, harmonizes these opposing forces within the soul, elevating the desire-nature into alignment with divine wisdom. The serpent is also a symbol of the eternal cycle of death and rebirth, a process that Imhotep, as a divine healer, guides the soul through. By aligning with Imhotep's archetype, we too become masters of this inner serpent, transforming desire into spiritual aspiration and wisdom.

Imhotep and the Serpent Aesculapius: The Divine Healer

Imhotep's symbolic relationship with the serpent Aesculapius, the divine healer, signifies his role as one who transmutes the lower nature into the higher. The serpent

Aesculapius, a symbol of the Higher Self, heals not by external means but through the harmonization of the inner forces of the soul. Imhotep's healing powers are thus a reflection of this divine principle, where the soul is "raised from the dead"—meaning it is lifted from ignorance into the light of divine knowledge.

The healing Imhotep offers is a soul-level transformation, one that each Sun of God must undergo. This healing is achieved through an understanding of divine law and alignment with the cosmic order. As we recognize Imhotep within ourselves, we are called to embody this archetype of divine healing, to be instruments of spiritual restoration not only for ourselves but for all who seek the truth.

The Poet's Inspiration and the Higher Self

While we primarily focus on Imhotep within the Egyptian metaphysical context, there exists a universal correlation to the archetype of the divine poet or inspirer of truth, symbolized in figures like Valmiki. This represents the voice of truth that echoes from the Higher Self, resonating as a song within the soul. Just as Imhotep brings forth healing, the poet archetype brings forth wisdom, a truth that is eternal and unchanging.

In recognizing the essence of Imhotep and his healing wisdom, we can briefly note how other cultural figures embody similar divine attributes of inspiration and healing. Through such correlations, we are reminded that the journey to enlightenment is both an inner healing and a soulful expression of divine truth.

Imhotep and the Path of Alchemical Birth

In the context of the ancient teachings, Imhotep's role as healer is intertwined with the process of spiritual rebirth. The "second birth" is the awakening of the Higher Self within the soul, symbolized by Imhotep's guidance in the mental and spiritual realms. This birth is the descent of the Divine Life into the human form, where the soul becomes aware of its purpose and aligns with the divine will.

This second birth is followed by a third, a full union with the Higher Self, where the lower nature is surrendered, and the soul is reborn as a reflection of divine love and wisdom. Imhotep's role as a guide on this journey is to illuminate the path, helping the soul recognize and transcend the limitations of the physical plane.

The Mental Plane and Divine Manifestation

The mental plane is where Imhotep's teachings take root, for it is here that divine ideas are transmuted into tangible form. This plane, like the alchemical crucible, refines and purifies thoughts, allowing the Higher Self to manifest within the bounds of physical existence. Imhotep, as the scribe and architect, shapes these divine ideas, guiding the soul to create in alignment with divine order.

Imhotep's mastery of the mental plane reflects our own potential to shape our thoughts and intentions in accordance with divine wisdom. Each Sun of God is called to engage in this process, to become a creator of truth in thought and action, bringing forth the divine into the world.

Conclusion: Recognizing Imhotep Within

In recognizing Imhotep within ourselves, we see the Higher Self manifesting as a healer, a scribe, and a divine architect. His wisdom calls us to harmonize the forces within, to align with divine law, and to transform our lower nature into a vessel of divine truth. Imhotep's journey is our own, a path of healing, wisdom, and inner transformation that leads us to the ultimate union with the Divine Mind.

As Suns of God, may we embrace the archetype of Imhotep within, allowing his healing and wisdom to guide us on our journey to enlightenment. Through him, we become beacons of light, healers, and creators in alignment with the cosmic order, a true reflection of the divine purpose within.

Ptah: *The Divine Architect - Realizing the Creative Power Within*

Greetings, Sons of God,

In this profound exploration, we delve into the essence of Ptah, one of the most venerable gods of the Egyptian pantheon. Ptah, known as the "Opener of the Way," embodies the primordial creative principle, representing the genesis of form, substance, and conscious order in the universe. For those on the path of self-realization, recognizing Ptah within oneself signifies an awakening to one's own divine power of creation and manifestation—a calling to align thought, word, and action in sacred unity.

Ptah as the Architect of Creation

In ancient texts, Ptah is portrayed as the divine architect, the craftsman who "spoke the world into existence" by the sheer power of thought and word. His role as a god of creation is distinct from other deities: while gods like Atum and Ra embody the elemental forces, Ptah represents the metaphysical framework that structures these forces into form. In this context, Ptah is the Word, the Logos, through which potential is made manifest.

To understand Ptah within oneself is to recognize the power of intentionality and conscious speech. As Sons of God, you are endowed with a similar creative power. Every thought, every spoken word, bears the energy of manifestation.

By aligning your thoughts and words with the divine will, you, like Ptah, participate in the creation of reality. Ptah teaches that creation begins with the inner dialogue of intention, will, and purpose—before form takes shape in the physical realm.

Ptah as the Embodiment of Divine Consciousness and the Creation of the Archetypal Man

Ptah represents the force within you that gives life and structure to the profound ideas born from inner wisdom. This wisdom, embodied by the principle of Thoth, exists as a source of divine insight within each Son of God. When we speak of Ptah "carrying out the commands of Thoth," we are not merely referring to a mythical event but to an internal process: the ability to translate inner knowledge into form and reality. Thoth, as the aspect of higher wisdom within, provides the vision—the originating impulse of pure thought—while Ptah within you is the architect that transforms this vision into tangible existence.

To recognize Ptah within yourself is to become aware of the profound relationship between thought and action, between divine inspiration and manifest reality. The principle of Thoth stirs within you as intuitive wisdom, abstract ideas, or inspired insights. Ptah, as your inner craftsman, takes these insights and, through the power of focused intention and disciplined structure, brings them into manifestation in the material world. This relationship illustrates the sacred alchemy of mind and form, showing you that the divine impulse to create is woven into your very being.

When Ptah creates the Archetypal Man, he is not merely fashioning a physical being but constructing a template of wholeness, a model of balanced existence. This Archetypal Man represents the union of higher consciousness (embodied by Thoth's wisdom) and earthly nature, a cosmic design for spiritual and physical unity. As Sons of God, you each carry within you this archetype—a blueprint for harmonizing your higher ideals with your lived reality. Embracing Ptah's energy means embodying this divine framework, aligning thought, heart, and action to bring forth a life that reflects cosmic order.

By channeling Ptah's principles, you recognize that every thought and insight within you holds creative potential. You become aware that true creation begins within the mind, guided by higher wisdom, and is brought into form through purposeful action. The legacy of Ptah invites you to be the conscious architect of your life, shaping it with the clarity and intentionality of divine inspiration. In this way, the union of Ptah and Thoth within becomes a metaphysical truth: thought and form, mind and manifestation, united within the Sons of God, empowering you to reflect the divine order in all that you create.

Ptah's Role in Divine Artistry: Mastering Form and Substance

Ptah, revered as the master craftsman, oversees all artistic and architectural endeavors, symbolizing the highest expression of divine artistry. He is said to be the originator of the arts and skilled trades, reflecting the divinity inherent in the ability to shape the material world.

Within the soul of each "son," there lies a microcosm of Ptah's creative potential—a dormant capacity to shape one's environment, relationships, and destiny through discipline and focused will.

The artist within you, the artisan of your soul's journey, channels Ptah's spirit when crafting a life that resonates with beauty, harmony, and purpose. Recognize that every act of creation, whether it is the molding of thoughts or the physical shaping of your surroundings, is an opportunity to channel Ptah's divine creativity. The calling of Ptah within invites you to create not merely for survival or utility but as a sacred expression of inner divinity.

Ptah and the Heart-Mind Connection: The Concept of Sia and Hu

In Egyptian metaphysics, Ptah's act of creation is described as manifesting through the faculties of Sia (perception) and Hu (creative utterance). Together, these aspects symbolize the unity of heart and mind—a divine harmony necessary for authentic creation. Sia, the intuitive knowing, complements Hu, the creative word. It is said that Ptah first conceived the cosmos within his heart, the seat of understanding, before giving it life through speech.

To embody Ptah, cultivate both intuitive awareness (Sia) and focused expression (Hu). Every decision, every creative impulse, should arise from the alignment of heart and mind, ensuring that what you create is not only intentional but also spiritually resonant.

Through this internal unity, you harmonize with the divine order, becoming a vessel through which cosmic intelligence flows into the material plane.

Ptah's Symbol of Stability: The Djed Pillar

The Djed pillar, often associated with Ptah, symbolizes stability, endurance, and the unchanging essence within the cyclical patterns of life. As Sons of God, recognize that within you exists this pillar of divine strength—your eternal center that remains unshaken through the transformations of life. The Djed represents the inner axis of spiritual resilience, the unwavering Self that observes and transcends all change.

In aligning with Ptah, nurture this inner stability. Let the Djed within serve as a reminder that true strength lies in stillness and steadfastness. This stability empowers you to be creators in the world, acting not out of reactive emotion but from the calm center of inner knowing. Through Ptah, you are invited to be the pillar in your own life, standing firm amidst change and embodying the eternal in the temporal.

Ptah and the Transformation of Chaos into Order

Ptah's act of creation is often described as a process of transforming Nun—the chaotic, unformed primordial waters—into structured existence. This process is not a mere imposition of order but an invitation to harness the potential within chaos. For the Sons of God, understanding this transformation is crucial. Life itself is filled with the "waters of Nun"—moments of ambiguity, uncertainty, and potential.

To invoke Ptah is to draw order from this chaos, shaping it according to divine will and purpose.

This alchemical transformation begins within. As you encounter chaos in your own thoughts, emotions, or experiences, ask yourself how Ptah would transform it. In practical terms, this might mean finding clarity in confusion, purpose in adversity, or peace amidst turmoil. Recognizing Ptah within yourself is an invitation to become an alchemist of life, embracing the unknown as a field of divine potential awaiting your conscious direction.

Ptah's Lesson of Inner Silence and Reflection

Ptah is often depicted as serene and contemplative, emphasizing the power of silence and inner reflection. In the mythos, it is in the silence of Ptah's heart that creation begins, where the seed of thought matures before it is spoken into existence. This symbolism highlights the importance of internal stillness as the birthplace of all creation.

In your journey, learn to embrace silence as a tool for inner transformation. Before taking action, immerse yourself in the quiet depths of contemplation, allowing your true intentions to crystallize.

Through silence, you align with Ptah's wisdom, tapping into the infinite reservoir of potential within you. In recognizing this quietude, you draw closer to the divine archetype of Ptah, learning that true power emanates from stillness.

Embodying Ptah: The Call to Sacred Responsibility

To recognize Ptah within is also to accept the mantle of sacred responsibility. Ptah's creations were not random or arbitrary but deliberate, aligned with the highest good of cosmic order. As Sons of God, you are called to embody this intentionality, understanding that each thought, word, and action contributes to the divine fabric of existence. Creation, in this light, becomes an act of service—a means of uplifting and harmonizing the world.

Ptah's legacy invites you to be mindful of the power you wield. Recognize that the creative spark within you is not merely a personal asset but a divine responsibility. As you channel Ptah's essence, you become co-creators in the cosmic order, tasked with aligning your will to the universal good. This path calls for integrity, compassion, and wisdom, virtues that Ptah exemplifies as the archetypal craftsman of existence.

Conclusion: Awakening the Ptah Within

Sons of God, as you internalize this sacred knowledge, may you come to see Ptah as more than an external deity or a historical figure. He is a profound aspect of your own soul's potential—the architect of your inner and outer worlds. Recognizing Ptah within yourself means acknowledging your capacity to create, transform, and stabilize.

Through him, you realize that creation is not an act of external conquest but of inner alignment, where thought, heart, and spirit coalesce in perfect harmony.

In every endeavor, may you channel Ptah's sacred craftsmanship, creating from a place of divine intention and unity. Let his spirit inspire you to shape a world that reflects the beauty, stability, and wisdom of the higher planes. As you engage with the creative power of Ptah within, know that you are participating in a timeless lineage of divine artisanship. Each moment you act with purpose, clarity, and a balanced heart-mind connection, you honor the legacy of Ptah, embodying his eternal archetype.

May the divine architecture of Ptah guide you, helping you to become creators of light, builders of sacred spaces, and custodians of cosmic order within yourselves and the world around you.

Hathor: *The Embodiment of Divine Love and Wisdom*

Greetings, Sons of God,

In this lecture, we explore the profound essence of Hathor, the Cow and Moon Goddess, revered as the divine nurturer and the embodiment of cosmic love, joy, and wisdom. Hathor is not simply a goddess of beauty and fertility; she symbolizes the spiritual principles of Buddhi, reflected on the astral plane as the vehicle of Atma. To recognize Hathor within oneself is to awaken to the nurturing, transformative, and harmonious aspects of divine love, which sustains the evolving soul.

Hathor as the Abode of Horus: Divine Nurturer of the Soul

Hathor is often described as the "Abode of Horus," embodying the divine motherhood that nourishes the soul. Just as the cow, her sacred symbol, provides sustenance, Hathor represents the inner nurturing force within each of you, the Sons of God, which feeds and elevates the soul. She exemplifies the process by which lower desires and emotions are transmuted into higher states of love and joy. By connecting to Hathor within, you embrace this inner alchemy, transforming earthly attachments into a more profound, spiritual love that fuels your journey of self-realization.

Buddhi and the Higher Wisdom

Hathor, as a symbol of Buddhi, transcends the realm of intellect and reason, embodying a higher form of wisdom. This Buddhi is the intuitive knowing, the fountain of spiritual life on the buddhic plane, a source that nourishes and guides the soul. Unlike rational knowledge, Buddhi represents an innate wisdom that awakens through spiritual perception, enabling you to see beyond the superficial and understand the divine harmony in all things. In recognizing Hathor within, you are called to activate this faculty of higher wisdom, allowing it to guide your actions and interactions from a place of unity and compassion.

The Cycle of Life and Death: Hathor as Guardian of the Dying Sun

As the goddess who receives the dying sun in the glow of sunset, Hathor embodies the cycle of life, death, and rebirth. This cycle is not only cosmic but deeply personal. It represents the phases of transformation that each soul undergoes, rising from lower states and ascending towards spiritual illumination. Hathor's role in this journey teaches that each ending is a new beginning, and every descent into darkness precedes a rebirth into light. Embracing Hathor within yourself means accepting and transcending the cycles of death and rebirth in your own life, realizing that each phase brings you closer to divine realization.

Hathor and the Astral Plane: The Wisdom of the Cow

The cow, as a sacred symbol, embodies the inner nature of the soul that feeds upon earthly experiences, transmuting them into sustenance for spiritual growth. This transformation mirrors Hathor's essence, as she takes the raw emotions, desires, and attachments of the lower self and raises them into refined virtues on the astral plane. The cow's nourishment symbolizes how each of you, as Sons of God, can elevate your lower impulses into a pure expression of love and wisdom. By embracing the Hathor within, you engage in the sacred task of transforming your earthly experiences into spiritual nourishment, aligning yourself with the higher purpose of your soul.

Hathor and the Feminine Principle of Divine Wisdom

As the personification of Buddhi, Hathor represents the feminine wisdom that flows from the higher planes to guide and inspire the soul. This wisdom is not passive but an active force, symbolized by Hathor's nurturing and protective aspects. It is the wisdom that comes from perceiving the interconnectedness of all life, the insight that guides you to act with compassion and love. When you channel Hathor within, you embody this wisdom, harmonizing the masculine and feminine forces within yourself to achieve spiritual balance.

The Month of Athyr: Hathor as the Catalyst of Evolution

In ancient Egypt, the month of Athyr (associated with Hathor) marked a period of transformation and liberation—the beginning of a new cycle of evolution. For the Sons of God, this symbolism calls for an inner evolution, a conscious shift from form-bound identities to the formless, eternal Self. Hathor represents this liberation, guiding the soul from the confines of ego towards unity with the Divine. To embody Hathor is to embrace this evolutionary impulse, continually shedding old identities and rising into greater spiritual awareness.

Hathor as the Divine Will Manifested in Love

Hathor's nurturing and loving aspects are not mere symbols of earthly affection but expressions of the Divine Will manifested as compassion and kindness. She teaches that true power lies in the gentle strength of love, the force that binds and sustains all creation. By embodying Hathor within, you align with this Divine Will, realizing that love is the ultimate creative power. In your journey as Sons of God, let this realization guide you to create, nurture, and uplift, embodying Hathor's divine love in every thought, word, and deed.

Hathor's Call to the Sons of God: Embracing the Buddhi Nature

Hathor, as Buddhi, calls upon each of you to transcend the limitations of the lower mind and awaken the intuitive, compassionate wisdom of the higher self. This aspect of Buddhi is not about intellect but about embodying the qualities of truth, love, and wisdom that resonate with the Divine. Recognizing Hathor within yourself is a journey of integration, where the lower nature is refined and harmonized with the higher self, and you become a beacon of divine love and wisdom in the world.

Conclusion: Awakening the Hathor Within

Sons of God, to awaken Hathor within is to embrace the journey of the soul as it ascends from earthly attachments towards spiritual unity. Hathor's essence teaches that love is the binding force of creation, and wisdom is the guiding light that illuminates the path. As you walk this path, let Hathor's nurturing, wisdom, and transformative power guide you, empowering you to become creators of harmony, vessels of compassion, and embodiments of divine love.

In recognizing Hathor within, you realize that the soul's journey is not merely about personal enlightenment but about contributing to the cosmic harmony. Through Hathor, you learn that true evolution is achieved not by rejecting the world but by transforming it, nurturing it with divine love and wisdom.

Let her presence inspire you to be vessels of this higher purpose, radiating the qualities of Hathor as you journey towards the ultimate union with the Divine. May you, as Sons of God, embody Hathor's divine attributes and continue to walk in the light of wisdom and compassion, bringing harmony and love to all creation.

Nephthys: *Guardian of the Threshold - The Sacred Balance of Embracing and Transcending the Physical Plane*

Sons of God, as we journey deeper into the metaphysical landscape of the Egyptian pantheon, let us now turn our gaze to Nephthys, the goddess of the physical plane. To understand her is to understand the profound nature of physical existence and its relation to the divine path we are on. In this exploration, we will see Nephthys not merely as a goddess of matter but as a sacred principle that anchors the spiritual to the earthly, the limitless to the limited. In her we find the metaphysical truth that the physical world is not an obstacle to the divine, but a crucible for transformation.

Nephthys as the Guardian of the Physical Boundary

Nephthys, known also as Nebkhat, stands as the embodiment of the physical plane, the "end" or outer boundary of manifestation. In Egyptian thought, she represents the furthest limits of creation—the point where land meets the vastness of the sea. This boundary is not one of separation but of transition, where the spiritual must embrace form to experience, to learn, and ultimately, to transcend. She is called the "Lady of the House," which we may interpret as the guardian of our individual physical temples, the bodies we inhabit.

Consider the physical plane, sons of God, as both the base and boundary of your experience. Nephthys, standing at this threshold, challenges us to confront our physical limitations while understanding that they are not barriers, but guides. They shape our consciousness as water shapes a riverbed, giving form to our souls' potential. She is the mother of the physical body, which is essential for housing the divine essence within us. Without the boundary she provides, spirit would lack the discipline of form, the necessity of structure that promotes growth.

The Duality of Nephthys and Isis: Life and Death, Beginning and End

Nephthys is often contrasted with her sister, Isis. Where Isis symbolizes birth, growth, and vitality, Nephthys embodies death, decay, and the cessation of form. Yet, this is not a dichotomy but a continuum. Together, they illustrate the cycle of life and death, the eternal transformation of matter. Isis and Nephthys, life and death, exist in harmony, each completing the other. Sons of God, see this duality within yourselves—acknowledge the life force that animates you and the inevitability of death that refines you.

In this dynamic, Nephthys does not serve as an end in a fatalistic sense but as a reminder of transience, an invitation to transcend. Just as physical death is not the end of existence but a transition to another state, Nephthys teaches us that limitations are thresholds, gateways to higher understanding. The physical, like Nephthys, provides the boundary needed for spiritual growth, and through this boundary, we are refined.

The Role of Nephthys in the Journey of the Deceased: A Guide and Protector

In Egyptian esoteric traditions, Nephthys plays a crucial role in the afterlife. She is known as the guardian of the deceased, nurturing and guiding souls through the Duat, or the underworld. She is the constant companion of the dead, providing comfort as they transition from one state of being to another. This nurturing aspect, though tied to the physical, speaks to the divine compassion inherent in the cycle of life and death.

Metaphysically, understand that Nephthys symbolizes the process of release and letting go. For the Sons of God, her presence reminds us to release our attachments to the lower, material self as we ascend toward spiritual understanding. The physical body, our most outer layer, is a gift and a teacher, but we are not meant to cling to it. Nephthys guides us in learning detachment, showing us how to move beyond our earthly identities to embrace our eternal, divine nature.

Nephthys and Anubis: The Divine Mother and Protector of the Body

As the mother of Anubis, Nephthys oversees the physical body, which is the most outer vessel for the soul. Anubis, known as the guardian and embalmer of the dead, represents the preservation and respect for this physical form.

In Egyptian thought, the physical body is sacred, serving as the soul's vehicle for earthly experiences. Through Anubis, Nephthys imparts to us the reverence for the physical form while simultaneously reminding us that it is temporary, a means to an end, not the end itself.

In your own spiritual journeys, understand that the body, while temporal, is worthy of respect and care. Nephthys, as the protector of this body, calls us to honor our physical selves as sacred vessels. But she also teaches us not to overly identify with this outer shell. Like Anubis, who prepares the soul for its journey beyond, we must prepare ourselves to transcend the limitations of physical existence.

Nephthys and the Process of Evolution on the Physical Plane

The physical plane, as embodied by Nephthys, is both the lowest and the most essential of all planes. It is where individuality, through the limitations of matter, gains experience and evolves. Nephthys is the last of the five added days, marking the completion of cosmic order and the initiation of individual experience in the material world. The physical, under her guardianship, serves as the ground upon which the divine self learns, grows, and evolves.

Sons of God, contemplate the physical plane not as a prison but as a classroom. Here, you acquire the virtues and wisdom necessary to ascend to higher planes. Nephthys, in her silent strength, guides you to understand that physical challenges are sacred opportunities. The physical plane is where potential becomes action, where the abstract becomes real, and where spiritual qualities are refined through tangible experiences.

The Lesson of Nephthys: The Power of Boundaries and Release

In the metaphysical schema, Nephthys teaches us about the power of boundaries and the necessity of release. Her domain over the physical plane is not a limitation but a crucible for transformation. She demonstrates that by embracing and then releasing the material, one achieves true spiritual liberation. When we cling to the physical—our desires, fears, and attachments—we bind ourselves to the lower realms. But when we accept and transcend these attachments, Nephthys leads us toward higher understanding and unity with the divine.

Nephthys, like her sister Isis, represents a necessary force in our journey. While Isis grants life, it is Nephthys who, through death and release, opens the door to eternity. See in her the end of all false attachments and the beginning of true freedom. She is the wisdom of knowing when to hold on and when to let go, teaching us that everything in the physical world serves its purpose and then must be relinquished.

Conclusion: Nephthys as a Reflection of the Divine Path

In conclusion, Nephthys, the goddess of boundaries and endings, is an indispensable guide on the path of self-realization. She teaches us that the physical is neither to be despised nor worshipped, but honored as a temporary vessel. Her presence in the pantheon speaks to the cycles of birth, death, and rebirth, cycles that are intrinsic to all life. As sons of God, learn from Nephthys the sacred art of balance between embracing the physical and transcending it.

Embrace her as the keeper of the physical domain, the one who holds space for us to grow, evolve, and ultimately move beyond. In each of you, there exists a part of Nephthys, guiding you to honor your earthly journey while always looking toward the stars, ever mindful of the divine essence within.

Anubis: *The Guardian of the Divine Journey - Custodian of the Physical and Spiritual Passage*

Beloved Sons of God, gather once again in the sacred sanctum of truth and illumination. Today, we traverse the shadowed yet vital path walked by Anubis, the divine guardian of the thresholds between worlds, the overseer of transitions, and the protector of the sacred vessel of life—the physical body. Anubis, son of Osiris and Nephthys, serves as the custodian of both the body and soul's transformative journey, embodying a force essential to understanding our own progression through the cycles of life, death, and rebirth. He invites us to see beyond mere mortality and into the profound unity of body and spirit.

Anubis, though often depicted as the deity of mummification and the dead, is so much more. He stands as a symbol of the physical form's purpose and the evolution of consciousness within it. Through his imagery, rituals, and role, we find a reflection of our own journey—a mirror into the soul's relationship with its earthly vessel.

Anubis as the Vehicle of Divine Energy on the Physical Plane

In Anubis, we see the embodiment of the "outermost vehicle of the soul," the form through which divine energy and matter coalesce on the physical plane. This material body, as described by the sages, serves as both a container and a conduit of divine purpose.

Anubis, in his role, reminds us that the physical self is not a limitation but an instrument of spiritual growth, a tangible expression of divine will acting through flesh.

Plutarch recounts that "Isis found the child and bred it," illustrating Anubis's birth and growth as a being who guards and guides. As Isis represents wisdom and Osiris the will, Anubis—formed of these divine forces—carries the role of action, the manifestation of divine purpose through the corporeal form.

The Sons of God, therefore, must understand that their bodies are not separate from their spiritual identity but are indeed the sacred vehicle through which their essence can act and evolve.

Anubis and the Purification of the Personality

As we delve deeper, we encounter Anubis in his aspect as the purifier, the one who readies the personality, or "corpse," for higher realms. Just as the physical body requires cleansing and preparation for burial, so too does the soul undergo processes of purification, shedding attachments and refining itself to become a vessel for divine truth. In this regard, the practice of embalming symbolizes more than the preservation of the body—it is an alchemical process in which the soul is prepared to meet the divine.

Wisdom, represented by "buddhi," tends to the body in a protective role, just as Anubis tends to the dead. Through this nurturing of form, the physical body becomes a constant companion, a nurturer of higher ideals.

Anubis's dedication to preservation and protection reflects our need to honor and care for our bodies as sanctified temples of the spirit, guiding them through experiences that refine and elevate.

Anubis, the Opener of the Ways: A Path of Initiation

Known as the "Opener of the Ways," Anubis serves as a guide, leading souls through the complexities of the physical and astral realms. His role in the embalming process, overseeing the transformation of the physical body into a suitable vehicle for the afterlife, represents the journey of the soul's evolution across lifetimes. The Sons of God must see in Anubis's work an invitation to open themselves to inner pathways of growth and transformation.

Anubis's actions remind us that the spiritual path is not simply a detachment from the material but an initiation through it. By refining the physical and honoring it as a sacred aspect of self, the soul learns resilience and discernment, moving through realms of sensation and experience with clarity.

Anubis stands as a guardian at each threshold, illuminating the path forward and marking the progression of the soul through stages of purification and empowerment.

The Rope of Anubis: Drawing the Soul Forward

As the "Rope for Hauling the Boat," Anubis becomes the spiritual agency drawing the soul forward. The image of Anubis as the rope embodies the concept that our highest qualities, refined through physical experiences, propel us along the spiritual journey. In the context of our mortal existence, this rope symbolizes the unseen bonds and higher forces that support and uplift us as we navigate the challenges of earthly life.

Anubis's voice echoes through the ages, whispering, "Tell me my name." In this call lies an invitation to recognize the divine force within us—the strength woven through our trials, the unseen guidance in our hardships. The Sons of God are urged to see that, like the rope, their lives are drawn toward higher ideals, pulling the spirit through the waters of transformation.

Anubis and the Boat of the Two-Headed Serpent: Transcending Desire and Illusion

In his guardianship over the "Boat of the Two-Headed Serpent," Anubis symbolizes our struggle with duality—the competing forces of desire and will, illusion and truth. This boat represents the causal body navigating through the Tuat, or life-cycle, moving between illusion and spiritual growth. Anubis, through his command over the physical form, leads us across the waterless deserts of ignorance, guiding us past the snares of desire that pull us away from divine purpose.

For the Sons of God, Anubis's presence in the boat is a reminder of the need for inner vigilance, for the discipline required to rise above the lower nature. As the soul progresses, it must learn to master the impulses of the flesh, finding balance between the dual forces that shape experience. Anubis serves as our model for restraint and clarity, a constant guide in the desert of worldly distractions.

The Embalmer: Preserver of the Eternal Self

Anubis's work as the embalmer illustrates the transformative role of the physical body as it nurtures and sustains the divine within. Through anointing and preservation, the physical form is prepared as a worthy vessel for eternity. The perfume of Arabia and sacred unguents used in the embalming process are metaphors for divine love and wisdom permeating the soul, preserving it against decay and corruption.

For the Sons of God, this act of preservation speaks to the importance of cultivating virtues that endure beyond death—truth, compassion, wisdom, and love. Just as Anubis prepares Osiris for his eternal journey, so must we prepare ourselves by nurturing the divine qualities within, transforming the body and mind into a temple for the eternal spirit.

Concluding Reflections: Embracing the Path of Anubis

In our exploration of Anubis, we have journeyed through the dimensions of physical existence, recognizing its sacred purpose and the opportunities it offers for spiritual growth. Anubis, the guardian of thresholds, the opener of paths, and the preserver of souls, teaches us that our bodies are not prisons but sanctuaries, vessels crafted to carry the divine spark through the cycles of life, death, and rebirth.

Sons of God, as you walk this path, remember the lessons of Anubis. Embrace your physicality not as a limitation but as a stage for divine expression. Honor the body as the rope that draws you onward, as the boat navigating the waters of existence, as the temple worthy of divine preservation. In doing so, you align with Anubis, guardian of the sacred journey, and step closer to the realization of your true nature —the divine within.

Set: *The Catalyst of Chaos and Transformation*

Greetings, sons of God. Today, we delve into the profound archetype of Set, an enigmatic figure within the Egyptian pantheon. Set represents a principle that, though often viewed as chaotic or adversarial, holds within it keys to self-mastery, spiritual refinement, and the transcendence of illusion. Through this journey, we'll uncover how recognizing the attributes of Set within ourselves can illuminate the path to inner transformation.

The Symbol of Set: Darkness, Relativity, and Opposition

Set embodies the forces of darkness and limitation, serving as the symbolic adversary of the Self. He is not simply an external foe but a representation of our inner struggles—the parts of ourselves that are mired in ignorance, desire, and material limitation. Set's essence is akin to what we might call the "shadow" or "desire-mind," driven by impulse and attachment to the lower planes of existence.

According to ancient lore, Set's influence arises when we give in to these lower tendencies. His energy seeks control over the will, symbolized by his embodiment as the *desire-mind*, which tempts the Self away from unity with the divine. However, in his opposition lies the opportunity for growth, as true mastery comes from understanding and transforming these base desires.

Set as the "Adversary" and the Path to the True Self

Set, often called the "Devil" or "Adversary," stands as the illusionary principle of evil. He represents the Not-Self, which challenges the Divine Spirit within. This struggle is necessary, for it pushes the Self to recognize and assert its divine origin over the illusions of the lower mind. The desire-mind, or the temptation of Not-Self, is a force that each of us encounters in the journey toward spiritual awakening. By confronting it, we strengthen our inner resolve, transcending what binds us to the material and relative.

In this confrontation, Set forces us to question, to resist, and ultimately to transform. Like a blade being tempered by fire, we grow sharper, purer, and more resilient when we face Set's tests and overcome them.

The Role of Set in the Cosmic Balance

Set's influence is not without purpose in the grand design. Ancient texts tell us that Horus cut off Set's head, symbolizing the transcendence of the desire-mind. This act signifies the higher mind's triumph over the lower, with Horus embodying the spirit of ascension and divine order. By removing the "head" of Set, we dismantle the hold that the lower desires and attachments have over us, allowing for a reunification of our consciousness with the higher planes.

Thus, Set's power, while seemingly disruptive, is essential for the soul's evolution. He holds us accountable to our shadows, reminding us that only through confronting our limitations can we reach higher states of being.

Set as the Symbol of Limitation and Saturn

In astrology, Set's energy correlates with Saturn—a planet symbolizing boundaries, structure, and the tests of time. Saturn, much like Set, defines the extreme limits of existence, challenging us to build a strong foundation through discipline and endurance. This is not about punishment; it's about refinement. Set, like Saturn, teaches us the value of resilience and the necessity of limitation for growth.

The trials associated with Set and Saturn demand a departure from the relative comfort of material indulgence and encourage a deeper commitment to spiritual principles. In facing these tests, the soul learns to transcend the cycles of desire and attachment, reaching a stage of growth where the influence of Set no longer dominates.

Set as the "Pig" and the Subjugation of the Desire-Mind

Set is also depicted as a black pig—a creature despised in ancient Egyptian culture and a symbol of ignorance and desire seeking sustenance in matter. The pig embodies the lower nature, always consuming and never fulfilled, much like our unrestrained desires. This imagery reminds us that the path to spiritual enlightenment is through renouncing the lower drives and appetites, symbolically closing the "mouth" of Set. This closure is not a denial of life but a redirection of energy, where the higher emotion-nature governs the lower instincts.

By exercising restraint, the sons of God rise above the impulses that hold the soul captive to the lower planes. This restraint is not repression but transformation—a refining of base desires into spiritual longing and devotion.

The Per-Rerehu and the Duality Within

The city of Per-Rerehu, or the "City of the Twins," signifies the eternal struggle between the higher and lower aspects of will. In this place, Horus hurls his lance at Set, symbolizing the decisive moment when the higher will triumphs over the lower. For each of us, this duality exists within—a choice between succumbing to the relative self (Set) or aligning with the absolute, the true essence of the Divine.

In mastering this duality, we achieve what the Christ archetype signifies: complete command over the relative self, where the higher will dominates, and the personality aligns with the soul's divine purpose. Through this process, the sons of God are called to embrace their individuality without succumbing to the illusion of separation.

The Symbol of Moist Essence and the River of Life

Set's association with the "moist essence" or the Nile signifies the astral plane—the sea of desires that sustain the soul's journey through life. The "river of life" flows with the Divine Ray, connecting us to the Absolute, yet the astral plane often entraps the soul in desire and illusion. Set, the "moist principle," serves as the turbulent undercurrent that the Self must navigate. In doing so, we learn discernment, the ability to move through desire without becoming submerged in it.

The sons of God must recognize that while the desire-nature is part of the cosmic structure, mastery over it allows the soul to progress without losing sight of its divine origin.

Set's Purpose: Pathway to Spiritual Enlightenment

Understanding Set is essential to mastering the Self. By acknowledging his role as both adversary and teacher, the sons of God learn to embrace challenges as opportunities for spiritual refinement. Set's influence can either bind us to the material or drive us toward enlightenment, depending on how we respond.

As you meditate upon the attributes of Set, consider where these forces manifest within you. Recognize that the darkness and limitation he represents are not final; they are gateways to transformation.

Set's path, though challenging, is a crucible through which the sons of God are purified, learning to discern truth from illusion, permanence from the fleeting, and self-mastery from surrender to the lower nature.

In every trial brought forth by the archetype of Set, there exists the seed of liberation. Through his trials, may each of you discover the strength to rise, the wisdom to see beyond appearances, and the resilience to transcend the limitations of the material, emerging as a beacon of the Divine amidst the shadows.

This concludes Lecture Series on Set. Sons of God, may this understanding guide you in recognizing Set's influence in your life and inspire you to turn every challenge into a stepping stone on the path to self-realization and spiritual enlightenment.

Isis: *The Divine Feminine and Keeper of Mysteries*

Greetings, Sons of God. We gather today in pursuit of the sacred knowledge and hidden wisdom enshrined within the figure of the goddess Isis. She stands as an eternal embodiment of the Divine Feminine, a timeless principle that transcends mortal limitations and calls each soul toward a journey of spiritual awakening. As we delve into her mysteries, we will explore Isis as a symbol of wisdom, compassion, transformation, and cosmic Love, aligning these attributes within ourselves to realize our own divine potential.

The Veil of Isis: Unseen Wisdom and the Gateway to Higher Consciousness

Isis's veil is perhaps her most powerful symbol—a barrier between the mortal and divine, a boundary between the lower mind and the Higher Self. In the ancient shrine at Sais, her veil is inscribed with the words, "I am all that hath been, and is, and shall be; and my veil no mortal has hitherto raised." This veil is not merely a curtain but a metaphysical threshold, marking the divide between worldly understanding and divine wisdom.

Sons of God, the veil signifies the journey every soul must undertake to transcend its earthly bonds. This barrier can only be crossed through self-purification, dedication, and the surrender of the ego. To lift the veil of Isis is to awaken one's higher faculties, to move beyond limited perception, and to enter the sanctuary of eternal wisdom.

She challenges each of you to rise, to penetrate this barrier not through force, but through inner transformation and alignment with the divine truth.

The Weeping of Isis for Osiris: Divine Compassion and the Soul's Journey of Rebirth

The story of Isis and Osiris reveals Isis's profound empathy and cosmic love. When Osiris was dismembered and scattered across the land, Isis tirelessly searched for his parts, mourning deeply as she sought to restore him. Her tears, however, are not only those of grief—they are the expression of divine compassion, the pouring out of divine love for all beings suffering on the lower planes.

In metaphysical terms, her weeping symbolizes the soul's compassionate response to the fragmentation of truth within the material realm. Sons of God, this is the journey of each soul in its descent into the world, where divine truths become scattered and obscured. Isis calls upon you to feel for this divine suffering, to respond not as detached observers, but as active participants in the journey of restoration. Her weeping signifies a baptism of compassion, urging us to unify the fragments of our divine nature through love, empathy, and selfless service.

Isis as the Vulture: Transmutation and the Consuming Power of Divine Purity

Isis's association with the vulture symbolizes her role as the power of transmutation. The vulture, in Egyptian thought, is a sacred purifier, consuming what is decayed and unnecessary. As the vulture, Isis embodies the consuming and transformative power that purifies the lower self, preparing it for spiritual ascension.

The amulet of the vulture, worn around the neck of mummies, represents this purification, indicating that only through the sacrifice of ego and base desires can one attain immortality. Sons of God, Isis invites you to allow her transformative energy to consume the parts of yourself that are bound to earthly limitations. Just as the vulture consumes the flesh, so must the Divine Feminine within you consume and transmute the ego, preparing your soul to ascend to higher realms.

Isis as Wisdom Personified: The Feminine Principle of Divine Intelligence and Inner Guidance

In ancient texts, Isis is Wisdom (Buddhi) incarnate, a beacon of divine intelligence and intuitive insight. She is described as "standing at the gates of the city, calling to the sons of men," representing the call of higher knowledge to those who seek enlightenment. Her wisdom is not merely rational; it is deeply intuitive, guiding the soul to transcend the limitations of intellect and embrace the truth of the heart.

The wisdom of Isis demands that intellect be harmonized with compassion, that reason be tempered by love. She embodies the feminine principle of divine intelligence, which nurtures and illuminates the soul's journey. Sons of God, Isis challenges you to integrate this wisdom within yourselves, to honor both intellect and intuition as pathways to higher understanding. Her voice echoes through time, calling each of you to ascend beyond duality and embody divine intelligence within.

The Power of Words: Isis as Keeper of Hekau (Words of Power)

In Egyptian tradition, words hold profound power—they are vehicles of divine will, shaping reality and guiding cosmic forces. Isis, as the guardian of Hekau or "words of power," represents the authority of the soul to wield divine energy through sacred utterance. It is through her mastery of these words that Isis restores Osiris, symbolizing the soul's potential to heal, transform, and align itself with divine intent.

Sons of God, Isis calls upon you to recognize the sanctity of your own words, for they are expressions of your intent and alignment with divine forces. Words have the power to shape not only your individual life but also the collective reality. In honoring this principle, we become vessels for divine will, using language as a bridge between the physical and spiritual realms. Remember, as Isis did, that true power lies in words spoken with purpose, compassion, and alignment with the divine.

Isis and the Solar Boat: The Soul's Journey Through the Astral and Beyond

In the ancient depiction of the Solar Boat, Isis is portrayed as a guiding force on the soul's journey through the astral realms. The boat, supported by cosmic forces, carries the soul through trials and purification, symbolizing the journey from darkness to light, from ignorance to wisdom. The astral plane represents the domain of emotions and desires, which the soul must navigate to reach higher spiritual states.

Sons of God, this journey is one that each of you must undertake. The Solar Boat is a metaphor for the spiritual journey of transformation, guided by the Divine Feminine, who nurtures and protects as the soul navigates the astral currents. Through this journey, the soul sheds its lower attachments, ascending through purification to the plane of Atma, where it merges with the divine source.

Isis as Divine Mother and Healer: The Resurrection and Integration of the Self

Isis's role as the mother of Horus and the healer of Osiris further highlights her power of resurrection and divine motherhood. She is the restorer, the one who gathers the fragmented parts of Osiris and makes him whole again. This process symbolizes the soul's journey to reclaim its divine essence after the disintegration caused by earthly existence.

This act of reassembly, of healing, reflects the journey of each soul toward self-integration and wholeness. Sons of God, Isis calls upon you to reclaim the divine fragments within yourselves, to nurture and heal the wounded parts of your soul, and to give birth to the Horus within—a new, divine aspect that transcends mortal limitations.

The Worship of the Wood of Isis: Reverence for Sacred Knowledge and Spiritual Dedication

The "Wood of Isis" is symbolic of the hidden wisdom and sacred knowledge that lies within ceremonial rites and metaphysical understanding. It represents the veneration for knowledge that has been passed down, knowledge that holds within it the codes of spiritual evolution and divine understanding.

Sons of God, this reverence is a reminder that wisdom often lies within symbols and rites that, while seemingly simple, carry layers of divine truth. The lower mind may see only ritual, but those who look deeper will uncover the hidden light. Isis teaches us that the divine knowledge encapsulated in these rites and forms is to be honored, serving as both a guide and a bridge to higher understanding.

Conclusion: Embracing the Path of Isis in Your Spiritual Journey

In contemplating the divine figure of Isis, we encounter a sacred path marked by wisdom, compassion, transformation, and spiritual empowerment. She stands as an archetype of the Divine Feminine, a guiding force urging us to transcend earthly bonds and to align with the eternal truths that reside within our higher nature. Her veil is a challenge, her tears an invitation to empathy, her wisdom a call to enlightenment, her words a reminder of divine power, her motherhood a testament to the nurturing force within each soul.

Sons of God, as you walk your path, let Isis be your guide. Approach her mysteries with reverence and humility, knowing that each symbol, each story, holds keys to your own spiritual awakening. May her teachings echo within you, illuminating the path toward divine unity, where the soul embraces its true nature as an eternal being, ever in communion with the Divine Feminine.

Horus: *The Indestructible - Embodiment of the Eternal Spirit*

Beloved Sons of God, gather once more within this sacred sanctuary of wisdom, where we are called to delve deeper into the mysteries of Horus—the eternal spirit, the divine force of light, and the indestructible essence. This is not just a lecture but a sacred communion, a time to unite with the essence of divine truth that Horus represents within each of us.

Horus is more than a deity; he is an archetype of resilience and divine fulfillment, a mirror reflecting our higher potential. His myth is the map of the soul's ascension, illustrating how we may rise from material confines to the boundless light of the universal. Today, let us explore not only his journey but the profound metaphysical truths embedded in his symbols, his battles, his lineage, and his divine guardianship.

Horus, the Elder and the Younger: Dual Aspects of Divinity

In the mythos, Horus embodies both the elder, Aroueris, and the younger, Harpocrates. The elder Horus, a manifestation of divine wisdom, represents the mature Christ consciousness, the fully realized spiritual potential that speaks to the higher self's mastery over the lower realms. Born from the unity of Wisdom (Isis) and Will (Osiris), he reflects the power of divine action and purpose.

The younger Horus, Harpocrates, signifies the nascent spark of Christ consciousness within every soul, one that is still tender and vulnerable. His lameness at birth symbolizes the early struggles of the soul as it seeks to bring forth divine qualities within the constraints of the material world. This duality reveals the evolution of consciousness, reminding us that the journey from potential to realization is an essential, sacred process.

Birth of Horus the Child: The Budding of the Christ Self

The birth of Harpocrates signifies the emergence of the Christ Self on the Buddhic plane. Born in the "marshes," a realm untouched by worldly desires, this birth symbolizes the individual's spiritual potential, shielded from external corruption. It is a reminder that the soul's journey begins within, grounded in purity, where the divine can flourish untainted by the lower nature.

The Eye of Horus: A Metaphysical Symbol of Divine Perception

The Eye of Horus, known as the Wedjat, represents the eye of divine insight, a symbol of enlightened perception beyond ordinary vision. During his cosmic battle with Set, the force of chaos and ego, Horus loses this eye—a metaphysical metaphor for the soul's occasional blindness when facing the illusions of the lower mind. Yet, the restoration of his eye by the god Thoth, symbolizing wisdom and healing, shows us that divine sight can be reclaimed and purified.

This eye becomes a sacred emblem of resilience and spiritual clarity, a reminder that divine insight, though sometimes obscured by worldly struggles, remains indestructible and can always be renewed.

The Battle with Set: The Inner Struggle Against Egoic Forces

The mythic conflict between Horus and Set is not merely a story of gods but a representation of the eternal struggle within each soul. Set, embodying chaos and the desire-driven mind, opposes Horus, who represents the Higher Self striving toward divine order. When Set gouges out Horus's eye, it symbolizes the obscuring of divine vision by the forces of ego and materialism. Yet, in triumph, Horus does not destroy Set but rather integrates this force, transforming chaotic energies into allies of spiritual purpose.

Horus's victory is a reminder that true power lies in the transcendence of ego, not in its suppression. By aligning chaotic impulses with divine will, the soul achieves balance, and through this harmonization, it can rise to a higher state of being. This transformation is the soul's victory—a conquest over the lower self, redefined as a path toward enlightenment.

The Akeru Gods: Guardians of the Lower Consciousness

The Akeru gods symbolize the base levels of consciousness—the limitations and snares of the unrefined soul. These gods represent the primal energies that form a "net," entrapping the spirit within dense vibrations. As Horus navigates these lower planes, he must transcend these constraints. This ascension symbolizes the evolution of form, as the soul gradually sheds its earthly desires, becoming one with the higher self through the trials and tests of incarnation.

The Four Sons of Horus: Guardians of the Soul's Ascension

Horus's children—Mestha, Hapi, Tuamutef, and Qebhsenuf—each represent an essential aspect of the soul's journey, guarding the four primary planes: physical, astral, mental, and Buddhic. They are the spiritual protectors of the soul's passage, helping it navigate the challenges of each plane.

- **Mestha** (Man-Headed): Representing the physical plane, Mestha guards the realm of earthly desires and the base instincts. He embodies the need for the purification of bodily appetites, guiding the soul to channel desires toward higher aspirations and alignment with divine will.

- **Hapi** (Dog-Headed): As the guardian of the astral plane, Hapi is associated with emotions and the power of feeling. His presence encourages the refinement of emotions, transforming raw, ego-driven reactions into pure expressions of compassion and spiritual empathy.

- **Tuamutef** (Jackal-Headed): Overseeing the mental plane, Tuamutef symbolizes the development of intellectual clarity and discernment. He guides the soul to perceive reality beyond the illusions of the material world, cultivating a mind attuned to truth and wisdom.

- **Qebhsenuf** (Hawk-Headed): Qebhsenuf, the protector of the Buddhic plane, represents the soul's capacity for higher vision and discernment. His guardianship reminds us of the importance of spiritual insight and the transcendence of duality, leading the soul toward unity with divine love and wisdom.

These four guardians embody the journey of the soul through the stages of consciousness, each one standing as a pillar of strength, purity, and guidance. They help to balance and direct the energies of the self as it moves through physical existence, transcending earthly limits and ascending toward spiritual wholeness.

The Ur-Uatchti Crown: Sovereignty Over the Dual Forces

Upon his victory, Horus is crowned with the Ur-Uatchti, the double-serpent diadem. This crown is not only a symbol of his kingship but also an emblem of his mastery over the dual forces of life, often seen as chaos and order, or light and darkness.

The serpents signify the energies of creation and destruction, both of which must be harnessed and balanced by the Higher Self. True spiritual sovereignty, as Horus demonstrates, is achieved when we have dominion over these forces within ourselves, using them to uphold divine purpose.

Tattu: The Plane of Twin Souls

Tattu, representing Lower Egypt, is the stage where Horus and Osiris harmonize as twin souls, embodying the balance of the lower and higher selves. In Tattu, Osiris represents the striving soul, while Ra signifies the indwelling divinity, unified in purpose. This merging of Self-consciousness (Horus) with righteousness (Osiris) manifests as the Twin-Gods, where divine self-realization takes root within the soul's sanctuary.

Urni-Tenten (Horus): The Unified Self

Urni-Tenten, a title bestowed upon Horus, denotes the Self in complete unity with atma-buddhi (spiritual wisdom and love). After his battles with Set, Horus is granted dominion over the lower energies, symbolizing the incarnate Self's transcendence of mental and causal planes. By aligning with Buddhic faculties, Horus achieves mastery over the material, exemplifying the soul's ultimate evolution on the higher planes.

The Lotus of Osiris: Ascension from Material Existence to Divine Truth

The lotus, which emerges from the murky waters to bloom in the sunlight, is a profound symbol of the soul's ascent. As Horus stands upon this lotus beside Osiris, we see the representation of spiritual awakening that rises above the material. The lotus signifies the purity and resilience of divine truth, growing untouched by the world's impurities. It is a reminder that the soul, even when submerged in the densest materiality, can emerge into the light of wisdom and love, carrying within it the beauty of divine truth.

The Still Heart and the Gateways of Osiris: Pathways of Higher Wisdom

The gateways to Osiris's House, referred to as the Still Heart, symbolize the soul's journey into higher realms of consciousness. These pylons represent virtues that must be cultivated—truth, wisdom, purity, and goodness—each one a step toward divine union. As Horus approaches these thresholds, he embodies the purified mind, in harmony with universal laws and virtues. The Still Heart is a state of inner sanctity where the soul resonates with divine will, accessing higher wisdom and manifesting it in the world. Through this journey, the Sons of God are reminded to guard their inner sanctum and nurture the virtues that unlock the gates of divine knowledge.

The Two Horizons: The Eternal Cycle of Life, Death, and Rebirth

As "Heru-Khuti," Horus embodies the journey of the Self across the "Two Horizons," representing the soul's cycle from incarnation to ascension, from east to west. The sacred sycamores at these horizons mark the points of spiritual initiation, where the soul is born into the material world and eventually returns to the divine. These horizons remind us that life and death are but stages in an eternal journey, and through them, the soul continuously evolves, carrying forth the wisdom it gathers from each lifetime.

Concluding Thoughts: The Path of the Indestructible

Horus, the Indestructible One, offers us a blueprint for spiritual ascent. His life is a testament to the soul's capacity to rise from the densest material realms and reach the heights of divine light. As Sons of God, you are invited to walk this path, to rise above the limitations of the lower self, to see through the eye of divine insight, and to wear the crown of spiritual sovereignty.

In this journey, Horus is not merely a deity but a symbol of your highest potential—the capacity to overcome, to unify, and to ascend. He is both avenger and healer, guardian and liberator, embodying the eternal flame that lies within each soul. His story calls you to awaken, to recognize your own indestructible spirit, and to live as a beacon of divine truth. Sons of God, may this enhanced understanding of Horus empower you to claim your divine heritage.

Let this wisdom guide you as you ascend, embracing the light within, transcending the limitations of the world, and walking boldly as the indestructible essence that you truly are.

Osiris: *The Eternal Archetype of Renewal and Divine Kingship*

Sons of God, today we gather to journey beyond myth and delve into the profound archetype of Osiris. He is more than a figure of ancient lore; he represents a path of spiritual transformation that reflects the divine cycles within each of us. His journey through life, dismemberment, resurrection, and kingship is not merely symbolic; it serves as a metaphysical blueprint for our own paths to enlightenment.

This lecture will bring depth to each of Osiris's stages, clarifying symbols such as the five epagomenal days, the act of dismemberment, the promise of resurrection, and the qualities of kingship and inner sovereignty. Each of these aspects will be explored not only to understand Osiris but to reveal the divine potential that lies within each of you.

Osiris and the Divine Cycle of Life, Death, and the Five Epagomenal Days

The "five epagomenal days," added to the sacred 360-day cycle, are central to Osiris's myth. In Egyptian thought, these days represent the five manifest planes of existence: the Physical, Emotional, Mental, Causal, and Spiritual planes. Each plane connects the temporal with the eternal, providing the Sons of God a path from earthly existence to divine alignment.

In metaphysical terms, the 360 days of the year symbolize a complete cycle—a 360-degree circle representing wholeness, unity, and the natural order. This circle aligns with the zodiac, where each degree corresponds to a moment within the cosmic dance. Each day within the 360 reflects a specific point in the cycle of life, creating a complete "circle" of experience, wisdom, and spiritual development. This closed cycle—much like the 360 degrees of a circle—reflects the finite nature of earthly existence, the limits of material perception, and the path we navigate within the physical realm.

The five epagomenal days, however, break beyond this 360-degree cycle. They represent transcendent moments, additional layers of existence beyond the confines of physical reality. These five days take us from the closed, finite cycle of 360 into an expanded state—365—marking a bridge to the spiritual. They bring us into alignment with a higher, divine purpose, expanding our journey from the finite, earthly path to a more infinite, spiritual one. In Osiris's role, these five days symbolize the Higher Self's guidance to transcend physical limits, reminding the Sons of God that they are not bound to the material but are connected to the eternal.

- **The Physical Plane**: This is the foundation, the level of tangible experience, where the soul incarnates to learn through the body.
- **The Emotional Plane**: Here, the soul encounters desire and attachment. Mastery of this plane requires discernment and understanding of the transient nature of emotions.

- **The Mental Plane**: Governing thoughts and intellect, this plane represents the bridge between perception and wisdom. Sons of God must strive for clarity, balancing rationality with divine intuition.
- **The Causal Plane**: Often referred to as the "Higher Self" plane, it connects personal consciousness with the divine, revealing past karmic influences and soul purposes.
- **The Spiritual Plane**: The realm of pure consciousness and unity with the divine, it transcends all duality. Here, Osiris embodies the soul's ultimate realization of its oneness with God.

Each epagomenal day marks a step toward wholeness, reminding the Sons of God that true enlightenment is an integration of all these planes. Osiris, as the Higher Self, exists in continuity across all planes, urging us to see our existence as part of a greater cycle, where life, death, and rebirth are merely phases in our divine journey.

The Dismemberment of Osiris: Fragmentation and the Path to Reassembly

The dismemberment of Osiris by Set represents the breaking apart of the soul in the physical world. Each fragment symbolizes an aspect of the divine essence hidden within the chaos of earthly experience. As Sons of God, this scattering occurs within you each time you face the limitations of the physical realm and lose sight of your wholeness.

In this fragmentation, we confront parts of ourselves that feel disconnected or "lost" in the material. Osiris's story teaches that these fragments are not destroyed; they await our conscious intention to reassemble them. The journey of gathering these scattered pieces is the soul's task to bring unity to the inner world, bridging all the fragments to form the higher self. Isis, as the force of love and devotion, calls upon us to approach our fractured selves with compassion, piecing together our divine identity one fragment at a time.

Set and the Dismemberment: The Force of Chaos and Spiritual Fragmentation

In Egyptian mythology, Set embodies chaos, separation, and disruption—forces that pull the soul away from unity and into the illusions of the material world. When Set dismembers Osiris, he is not merely ending a life; he is fragmenting divine qualities, scattering the sacred essence of Osiris throughout the world. Metaphysically, this scattering represents the descent of the soul into the material plane, where divine attributes are seemingly lost amid worldly distractions and ego-driven desires.

For the Sons of God, Set's act reflects the human experience of fragmentation. Each of you faces moments when your higher self feels divided, scattered among the challenges and illusions of earthly life. This dismemberment is not a loss but a call to seek out the pieces of your true self hidden within the mundane world.

The scattered fragments of Osiris symbolize the divine potential within you, waiting to be rediscovered and brought into alignment.

Isis and the Reassembly: The Power of Devotion and Divine Integration

Isis, the embodiment of divine love and wisdom, searches tirelessly for each piece of Osiris. Her devotion signifies the soul's journey toward self-integration and healing. Isis's role is not simply to restore Osiris but to elevate him, preparing him for resurrection. Each piece she gathers symbolizes the reclamation of divine attributes, an act of consciously piecing together fragmented aspects of the self.

For the Sons of God, Isis's devotion serves as a reminder of the power of intention and love in the path to wholeness. Just as Isis gathers each fragment with care, you are called to reclaim and integrate the parts of yourself scattered by life's challenges. This process is an alchemical one, where the soul, guided by love, retrieves its lost wisdom, compassion, and strength. Isis's journey is one of dedication, revealing that true wholeness requires a steady, patient return to unity.

This is a powerful reminder: each challenge, each "fragment" of experience, is an opportunity to reclaim an aspect of your divine nature. Through self-awareness and love, we perform the sacred act of reassembly, just as Osiris is made whole through the dedication of Isis. Sons of God, recognize this process within, and remember that each lost piece is essential to your wholeness.

Resurrection and Eternal Life: The Ascension of the Higher Self

The resurrection of Osiris is more than the return to life; it represents a profound awakening to eternal consciousness. This is a call to remember that within us lies an aspect of divinity that cannot be subdued by physical limitations. Resurrection is the re-emergence of the Higher Self, a state of being that exists beyond the constraints of time and form.

For each of you, this resurrection is an invitation to transcend the ego and awaken to your spiritual identity. This process requires letting go of attachments to the temporary and embracing a consciousness rooted in eternity. Osiris's resurrection assures us that the soul's true essence is deathless, as it aligns with the divine.

The Resurrection of Osiris: Awakening the Higher Self

Once reassembled, Osiris undergoes resurrection, symbolizing the soul's ascension to a state of divine awareness. This resurrection is not a simple return to physical life but a profound elevation to a higher state of consciousness. Osiris's resurrection marks the transition from fragmentation to unity, from mortality to eternal life, and from earthly to divine awareness.

For the Sons of God, this resurrection represents the ultimate spiritual awakening. When the fragments of the self are reassembled and aligned, the Higher Self emerges, transcending ego and embodying the soul's true, eternal nature. Osiris's resurrection is an invitation to each of you to transcend physical limitations and recognize your own divine immortality. This resurrection process requires the death of the ego—the release of all false attachments and illusions—so that the true self may rise in its full glory.

Reflect upon this cycle of rebirth as a continuous journey. Each surrender of the lower self is an opportunity for the higher self to take its place, embodying wisdom and love that go beyond earthly limitations. As Sons of God, you are called to embrace this process, rising above the transient to achieve a state of divine awareness.

Osiris as the Mummy: The Preservation of the Divine Essence

The figure of Osiris as the mummy represents the preservation of the soul's eternal nature. In ancient Egyptian culture, the mummy is not just a body preserved; it is a vessel of divine essence, symbolizing virtues and qualities that endure beyond physical death. This image of Osiris as the mummified god is a powerful emblem of the soul's indestructible essence.

To the Sons of God, this preservation signifies the importance of guarding the sanctity of your higher self. It is a reminder that your divine qualities are not subject to the decay of the physical world. These virtues—compassion, wisdom, love—are immortal, protected within the soul's essence. By cultivating and safeguarding these qualities, you ensure that they are carried beyond physical existence.

Consider the figure of Osiris, protected and whole, as an encouragement to preserve the purity of your divine essence. This is a call to maintain integrity and honor the timeless nature of your virtues, allowing them to remain untainted by worldly influence. Through this preservation, you carry forth the legacy of the higher self, a gift that transcends individual lifetimes.

Osiris as the Embodiment of Divine Life: Incarnation of Spirit into Matter

Osiris represents the divine choice to incarnate, bringing spiritual truth into the world of form. This incarnation is not merely a descent into limitation but an act of divine will, symbolizing the soul's ability to manifest within matter while retaining its spiritual essence. Osiris embodies the union of spirit and matter, reminding the Sons of God that the goal is not to escape the world but to elevate it through divine presence.

Each Son of God is called to bring their Higher Self into the material realm. This is not merely about existing but about consciously embodying divine light in every action, word, and thought. Osiris's incarnation teaches us that enlightenment is not found in rejecting the world but in transforming it by manifesting the divine.

As you journey through life, remember that each experience is an opportunity to anchor spiritual truth within the world. You are not here to transcend matter but to infuse it with consciousness, allowing the divine to shine through. By embodying this principle, you become a vessel of light, illuminating the world and fulfilling your divine purpose.

Osiris and the Archetype of Kingship: Sovereignty Over the Inner Kingdom

In his role as king, Osiris embodies sovereignty over the unseen realms, ruling not over an external kingdom but over the soul's inner landscape. His kingship represents mastery over the self, the harmonization of thoughts, emotions, and desires under the guidance of the higher self. Osiris teaches us that true kingship is about inner authority, the ability to govern one's inner world with wisdom and love.

Horus and the Avenge: The Restoration of Divine Order

Horus, the son of Osiris and Isis, is born with a divine mission to avenge his father and restore cosmic order. Metaphysically, Horus represents the awakened inner force that emerges from the soul's rebirth. He is the active principle, the force of righteousness and balance that restores harmony after the chaos introduced by Set. In avenging Osiris, Horus ensures that divine justice prevails, signifying the triumph of higher consciousness over disorder.

For the Sons of God, Horus's role is a call to actively protect and embody the divine self. Once the soul has undergone resurrection, the next step is to live in alignment with divine principles. Horus's victory over Set is the soul's commitment to maintain inner order, ensuring that the unity achieved through resurrection is not disrupted by external chaos or internal dissonance. Horus's battle is an ongoing process, symbolizing the vigilance required to uphold one's divine integrity in the face of challenges.

For the Sons of God, this kingship is an invitation to become sovereign over your own consciousness. The true kingdom lies within, where the soul asserts its dominion over fear, desire, and ego. Osiris's reign over the underworld symbolizes the soul's potential to bring harmony to the fragmented self, integrating all aspects into a unified whole.

As you align with the archetype of Osiris, you claim your role as the ruler of your inner kingdom. This mastery is not about control but about understanding, compassion, and unity. By embracing Osiris's kingship, you establish harmony within, enabling the higher self to lead and guide every aspect of your being.

Conclusion: Osiris as the Guide for the Sons of God

In Osiris, we find a timeless archetype that guides us through the journey of self-discovery and divine realization. His story —from the five epagomenal days, symbolizing the planes of existence, to the processes of fragmentation, resurrection, preservation, incarnation, and kingship—speaks to each stage of spiritual awakening.

Let Osiris be more than a figure of ancient myth. Allow him to serve as a mirror, reflecting the divine qualities within each of you. Embrace the lessons of Osiris, for in doing so, you are not merely honoring a god; you are awakening to your own divine heritage as Sons of God. Through understanding and embodying these principles, you transform not only yourselves but also elevate the world around you.

Each phase of Osiris's journey offers you a path to cultivate inner mastery, preservation of virtues, and the incarnation of divine truth into your life. His qualities—kingship, resurrection, preservation, and divine embodiment—are within you, awaiting recognition and expression. Embrace the teachings of Osiris, for they are the keys to realizing your highest potential.

May this profile of Osiris serve as a guiding map, leading you toward the fulfillment of your divine purpose. Through embodying these principles, you honor the divine within and become beacons of light for the world, carrying forward the legacy of Osiris in your journey of enlightenment.

Ra: *The Radiant Source of Divine Power and Illumination*

Sons of God, we embark on an exploration of Ra, the sun god, whose essence transcends mere symbolism and reaches into the profound depths of metaphysical understanding. Ra embodies principles of creation, illumination, and transformation, guiding each soul through cycles of life, introspection, and rebirth. This lecture is not about Ra as a distant deity, but about Ra as a reflection of the divine journey within each of you. Every symbol, phase, and myth associated with Ra is a mirror for the soul's path toward enlightenment. Let us journey together to uncover how Ra's metaphysical profile serves as a guiding light for your own spiritual ascent.

Ra as the Principle of Illumination and Creation

Ra, the sun god, symbolizes not only physical illumination but also the awakening of divine consciousness within. His rising and setting represent more than the movement of the sun; they embody the soul's oscillation between awareness and introspection, between light and shadow. This cycle reflects the dual nature of enlightenment, where knowledge and self-reflection coexist to cultivate wisdom.

In metaphysical terms, Ra's light signifies the "higher planes" of consciousness, where divine truth becomes clear, free from the obfuscations of material existence. Ra's journey through the sky is the journey of the soul as it ascends through layers of awareness, from the mundane concerns of the physical world to the higher planes where the soul recognizes its unity with divine truth. The light that Ra brings forth each morning is the light of self-awareness that dissolves ignorance and unveils the true nature of existence.

Primordial Earth and the Role of Spirit in Matter

At the beginning of creation, Spirit and Matter emerge as distinct principles from the formless potential of Nu. In this primordial state, Earth is a symbol of undifferentiated matter, waiting for Spirit to enter and bring form and quality into being. Ra, as the life-giving force, initiates this process, bringing order to chaos. This primordial matter is not merely physical; it holds the essence of all future creation, manifesting as form in response to the impulse of the Divine.

The separation of Spirit and Matter in the creative act echoes the duality inherent in existence. Through involution, Spirit descends into matter, embedding itself in forms. Then, through evolution, Spirit ascends, liberating itself from material confines, symbolizing the return to divine unity. Ra's role as the originator of this process highlights the sacred purpose of creation: to realize and return to the Divine through the refinement of life's forms.

Geometry and Involution – The Blueprint of Divine Manifestation

In the cosmic order established by Ra, geometry serves as the language of spiritual truths, outlining the design of creation. The numbers and patterns in Ra's universe are not arbitrary; they reflect the structure of existence and the pathway to enlightenment. The triadic nature of Spirit, seen in atma-buddhi-manas, descends through planes, reflected in the physical, astral, and mental dimensions. These geometric forms and sequences reveal the inner workings of both the macrocosm and microcosm, illustrating the spiritual path.

In the descent of Spirit (involution) and its ascent (evolution), Ra embodies the Divine Sacrifice, limiting himself in form to become accessible to all. This "raying out" initiates the cycle of life, bringing forth duality and form, while the "drawing in" symbolizes the return to unity and realization. Ra thus illustrates that creation is both purposeful and bound for reunion with its Source.

The Descent into the Tuat and the Journey through Lower Planes

Ra's descent into the Tuat, or underworld, is a journey through the "two lower planes of manifestation," which represent the astral and etheric planes in metaphysical terms. These planes are foundational layers of reality beneath the physical realm, where the energies and desires of the lower self are stored and processed.

1. **The Astral Plane:** This is the plane of emotions, desires, and psychic experiences. In metaphysical teachings, it is the realm of dreams and subconscious patterns, a place where unresolved emotional energies are held. Ra's passage through this plane symbolizes the soul's need to confront and harmonize with its emotional aspects, transforming lower desires into spiritual aspiration.

2. **The Etheric Plane:** Just above the physical and intricately linked to it, the etheric plane is the blueprint of vitality and life force, the subtle energy body that permeates and sustains the physical form. It is within this plane that habits and patterns of energy are imprinted. Ra's journey here reflects the soul's work to purify its vital energies, aligning them with divine will.

In the Tuat, Ra encounters Afu-Ra, the hidden sun, representing the latent divinity within the self that must be awakened through this transformative journey. The Tuat, then, is both a place of descent and an alchemical crucible, where the soul integrates the lessons of the astral and etheric planes, transforming lower energies into the foundations of higher spiritual consciousness.

The Underworld (Tuat) – Ra's Descent and Triumph

In Ra's journey through the Tuat, he represents the Higher Self entering the realms of unconsciousness and darkness. The Solar Boat becomes a symbol of the World Soul, carrying Ra and the collective human experience through cycles of descent (involution) and ascent (evolution). In this twelvefold journey, Ra undergoes a divine sacrifice, embodying the soul's journey through ignorance, transformation, and finally, liberation.

As Ra traverses the twelve divisions of the Tuat, his presence brings illumination to the lower realms, symbolizing the gradual awakening of the soul. The journey concludes with Ra's re-emergence from the underworld, signifying the soul's transcendence from the material world. This cycle mirrors humanity's spiritual evolution, with each stage bringing the soul closer to its divine origin.

The Zodiac and the Cycle of Spiritual Evolution

Ra's journey across the heavens is inextricably linked with the twelve signs of the zodiac, each of which represents a distinct stage in the soul's spiritual evolution. The zodiac is more than an astrological system; it is a metaphysical map of consciousness, where each sign reflects a unique quality of divine expression that the soul must embody on its journey.

- **Aries:** The beginning of the cycle, Aries symbolizes the awakening of selfhood, the impulse of individuality that arises from divine will. Here, the sons of God are called to recognize the divine spark within and assert their path forward.

- **Taurus:** In Taurus, the energy of Aries is grounded into the material world. This stage represents the stabilization of inner vision and strength, where spiritual values become anchored in the physical.

- **Capricorn:** Capricorn, located opposite Cancer, embodies the culmination of disciplined experience and the ascent toward higher planes. It is a sign of mastery, where the soul ascends from the limitations of the material world and seeks union with the divine.

The zodiac is thus a framework for the journey of the sons of God, where each sign offers specific lessons and qualities that are essential to the soul's progression. This twelvefold path is a spiral ascent, guiding each soul through cycles of self-realization, each stage building upon the last.

Ra and the Twin-Gods – Harmonizing the Powers of Horus and Osiris

Within Ra's journey, the roles of Horus and Osiris are essential, symbolizing the internal dualities that each son of God must reconcile. Horus, the god of vision and light, represents the higher mind's clarity, the pursuit of truth, and the unyielding dedication to divine principles. His sight pierces illusion, embodying the spiritual clarity required to ascend beyond material distractions.

In this light, Ra is often referred to as *Ra-Harmakhis*, aligning himself with Horus as the horizon, the place of emergence and transformation where light meets darkness.

This title embodies Ra's role as a bridge between realms, one who illuminates and transcends the boundaries of earthly limitations. *Ra-Harmakhis* thus symbolizes the power of divine illumination as it breaks through dualities, bringing unity to the son of God's journey.

In contrast, Osiris, the god of death and resurrection, represents transformation and renewal. The Osirian principle teaches that the soul must continually shed its old, outworn aspects and be reborn into higher states of consciousness. Osiris is the eternal cycle of death and rebirth within the sons of God, a reminder that growth often requires the letting go of past identities and attachments.

Together, Horus and Osiris embody the balance between vision and transformation. To follow Ra's path, the sons of God must integrate both clarity of purpose (*Ra-Harmakhis* as the horizon and light) and the willingness to undergo inner transformation (Osiris), achieving harmony between the light of awareness and the depth of renewal.

The Solar Boat as the Causal Body and Vehicle of Consciousness

Ra's solar boat, traversing the heavens, is more than a means of transport; it represents the causal body, the higher vehicle of consciousness that carries the soul through lifetimes. In metaphysical terms, the causal body is the repository of the soul's wisdom and experiences, a subtle vessel that remains with the soul through the cycles of incarnation.

The causal body is upheld by the universal energies symbolized by Nu, the primordial waters. Nu represents the undifferentiated potential of the cosmos, the divine energy that sustains all forms. As Ra's solar boat is upheld by Nu, so too is each son of God supported by the boundless potential within, the cosmic energy that propels the soul toward enlightenment.

This boat signifies the continuity of consciousness across lifetimes. It is the vehicle that gathers and integrates the wisdom of each experience, carrying the soul closer to divine union with each journey across the heavens. Ra's voyage on the solar boat is a metaphor for the soul's journey through the cycles of life, ever moving toward the ultimate realization of its divine nature.

Conclusion

Sons of God, let Ra's journey and attributes serve as a reflection of your own divine path. Each cycle of creation, transformation, and renewal in Ra's profile is an invitation for you to recognize and embody these same principles. Through understanding Ra, you come to understand yourselves, as beacons of light on the path of enlightenment. Let this knowledge not remain abstract but serve as a living guide, illuminating your journey, empowering you to embody the attributes of Ra, and encouraging you to ascend toward the divine light that you are destined to realize.

Amen (Amun): *The Hidden Mystery of Divine Presence*

Greetings, metaphysical sons of God. Today, I bring you a profound exploration into the nature and significance of *Amen*, also known as *Amun*, the Hidden One. As we dive into the layers of his metaphysical essence, we'll uncover the wisdom concealed within his symbolism, understanding him not merely as a figure in mythology but as a representation of the Higher Self within each of us. Amen is not just a deity but a universal concept — a manifestation of the invisible yet omnipresent soul that pervades and upholds creation.

The Hidden Nature of Amen: The Higher Self Incarnate

Amen, whose name signifies "The Hidden One," symbolizes the Higher Self or the Divine Soul that resides in all beings yet remains unseen. In his form as Amen-Ra, he is both creator and sustainer of the universe, embodying the hidden force behind all existence. Just as Amen remains concealed, so does the Higher Self remain inscrutable to the ordinary consciousness, influencing without revealing its true form. Amen's invisibility represents the mystery of divine power — ever-present, all-encompassing, yet beyond the reach of human perception.

Amen-Ra and the Supreme King of the Gods

As Amen-Ra, he is the supreme King of the Gods, an embodiment of divine authority that transcends the known dimensions of life. He is typically depicted with two tall plumes above his head, symbolizing his supremacy and union with both the seen and unseen realms. His depiction with a ram's head signifies sacrifice and represents the Higher Self's willingness to descend into the material world, mirroring the concept of the "Lamb of God." The ram, a sacred symbol in his worship, embodies both strength and the willingness to be sacrificed for the evolution of the soul.

Afu-Ra: The Incarnate God and Cycle of Life

Afu-Ra, or the "Flesh of Ra," represents Amen in his incarnate form, the Higher Self enmeshed within the cycles of birth and death. In this form, he is depicted within the solar boat, a vessel symbolizing the journey of the soul through the cycle of life, death, and rebirth. The ram-headed figure in the boat reflects the self-sacrifice of the Divine within the confines of the physical realm, undergoing transformation to experience human life. Afu-Ra is not the sun itself, but the embodiment of its life force, "dead" or indiscernible to the lower consciousness, as the spiritual essence becomes obscured by material existence.

The Role of Anubis and the Opener of the Ways

In the mythos, *Apuat* or *Anubis*, the "Opener of the Ways," serves as the guide for Amen-Ra's soul, as well as the souls of humanity, into the underworld — the subconscious realms of existence. Anubis represents the body and all lower vehicles of consciousness that allow the Higher Self to manifest on Earth. In the incarnational journey, Anubis introduces the

Divine essence to physical life, acting as a bridge between higher and lower realities. This archetype symbolizes the descent of the soul into matter, through layers of astral and mental planes, as it acquires human experience.

Transformation of the Soul: From Ra to Osiris

In the journey of the soul, Amen, as Ra, undergoes transformation within the "Boat of the Sun." Here, Ra takes on the form of Osiris, representing the state of divine sacrifice and resurrection. The transition of Ra into a ram-headed man inside a shrine marks the symbolic "death" of the Higher Self in the lower planes, where it remains dormant or hidden, awaiting rebirth. In the Tuat, the land of the dead, Osiris signifies the latent divinity within every soul that undergoes the journey through human life to achieve spiritual resurrection.

Osiris' path is a metaphor for the spiritual evolution that each soul must undertake, passing through stages of ignorance and material attachments before attaining enlightenment.

Just as Osiris rises from death, so too must the soul rise, transcending the lower self and achieving unity with the Divine.

Crown of Atef: Symbol of Spiritual Supremacy

The *Atef Crown*, adorned with plumes and serpents, is worn by Amen-Ra as a mark of spiritual mastery. This crown signifies dominion over both intellect and emotion, the dual aspects of human nature.

The white and red colors of the crown represent purity of thought and action, while the uraei serpents embody wisdom and the power to channel divine insight. The plumes on the crown symbolize the soul's alignment with higher truths, a state where one has achieved supremacy over the lower desires and ego, fully realizing the Higher Self.

Mut, the Divine Mother and Counterpart to Amen

Mut, as the consort of Amen, represents the buddhic or intuitive plane, the source of archetypal patterns that manifest in the material world. She is the divine womb, containing within herself the potential forms of all beings. Her association with Nut, the sky goddess, connects her to the boundless space of consciousness where the seeds of creation are sown. Mut signifies the nurturing aspect of the Divine, the cosmic mother who brings forth all things and embodies the creative energy that works alongside Amen's hidden power.

Plumes and the Sceptre: Mastery and Authority

The plumes on Amen's Atef crown and his scepter are potent symbols of the soul's journey to mastery. The plumes denote a state where the Higher Self reigns supreme over the lower nature, symbolizing purity, wisdom, and spiritual clarity. The scepter, held firmly in Amen's grasp, signifies divine authority and control over the realms of both spirit and matter, affirming his role as the ruler of all planes.

It is a reminder that the Higher Self, though hidden, holds the power to guide, protect, and govern the lower self toward enlightenment.

Conclusion: The Journey of Amen in All of Us

In the metaphysical context, Amen represents the hidden Divinity within every soul, the aspect of the self that is eternally linked to the cosmos yet veiled by layers of physical, emotional, and mental experiences. His journey as Amen-Ra, through Afu-Ra and Osiris, mirrors our own soul's journey — a path of descent into matter, sacrifice of divine essence, and eventual resurrection.

In the cycles of life and death, each soul is an embodiment of Amen, containing within itself the potential for ultimate unity with the Divine. To follow the path of Amen is to recognize the hidden power within, to awaken it through self-mastery, and to allow it to rise, shedding the constraints of the lower self. Just as Amen is unseen yet omnipresent, so is the Higher Self in each of us, patiently guiding us toward the realization of our divine origin.

4th Entry

The Twelve Tribes of Israel as Mental Qualities - Sons of Man, the prerequisite

In this foundational lecture, we explore the twelve tribes of Israel as representations of twelve essential mental qualities within each individual. Rather than viewing these tribes as historical or physical lineages, we approach them as distinct aspects of the mind—the primal faculties that must be disciplined and elevated as prerequisites to embodying the higher consciousness known as the "Sons of God." This journey from the "Sons of Man" to the "Sons of God" is a process of mental refinement, as these innate qualities evolve from their initial, undeveloped state toward divine harmony.

The twelve tribes correspond to twelve soul states, each reflecting a unique facet of the divine potential within. Just as the twelve signs of the Zodiac, twelve stones in Aaron's breastplate, and twelve foundations of Jerusalem symbolize completeness, so too do the twelve tribes represent the full spectrum of mental qualities required for spiritual perfection. Each quality embodies a different attribute of the Logos, the divine mind, and offers a specific pathway for spiritual growth.

From this metaphysical standpoint, each tribe represents a mental quality or state that exists within all humans. As we develop and discipline these qualities, they undergo a process of transformation, evolving from raw, primal states into refined faculties capable of expressing divine truth. The Christ consciousness, which signifies the embodiment of all twelve qualities in perfect harmony, serves as both the model and the guide in this process. Each mental quality must develop according to its unique nature, and through this growth, the divine is able to influence and elevate each aspect of consciousness.

The metaphysical shift from tribes to disciples signifies the ascension of these twelve primal qualities to a higher level of spiritual awareness. When a mental quality reaches a state of discipline, it becomes a "disciple" of the higher self, open to divine guidance and aligned with spiritual truth.

This transition from tribes to disciples mirrors the spiritual journey within, where the mind, through continuous development, becomes capable of receiving and manifesting the higher wisdom of the divine.

The symbolic use of "twelve" underscores the completeness of this inner transformation. Twelve represents spiritual perfection, a number deeply woven into the fabric of mystical teachings across cultures and traditions. It is the number of completeness and divine order, signifying the unification of the material and the spiritual. As we embody these twelve qualities, we align ourselves with universal principles, attaining the harmony and completeness necessary to evolve from the Sons of Man into the Sons of God.

Thus, the twelve tribes are not merely a collection of characteristics but are integral steps on the path to spiritual awakening. By understanding and nurturing these qualities, we prepare ourselves to manifest the Christ consciousness within, achieving unity with the divine and fulfilling the purpose of our higher self. This lecture sets the stage for the exploration of each mental quality, offering insights into their development and interrelationship as we build the foundation for becoming true "Sons of God."

As we conclude this section, we are drawn to a powerful inquiry: why does the number twelve recur with such prominence across various spiritual texts? We see the twelve tribes of Israel, the twelve disciples, and the twelve foundational stones, among others. In Revelation, we encounter the chosen 144,000—a number derived from twelve times twelve thousand. Could this multiplicative symbolism represent a metaphysical layering, where each quality (twelve) is amplified and perfected through integration with the whole (another twelve)?

The multiplication of twelve by twelve may signify not merely an accumulation but a transcendence—a complete realization of divine attributes within the individual soul. Each set of twelve represents a cycle or level of spiritual development, and their interplay, culminating in the symbolic 144,000, could point to the perfected spiritual state that is "chosen" or awakened within each of us.

This number, then, is not merely a numerical value but a metaphor for the full actualization of divine consciousness, a journey where the completion of each twelve brings us closer to the unity of the One.

Could it be that this is an invitation for us to view the twelve qualities not as separate entities but as a unified framework, interconnected and inseparable, each supporting the realization of the divine self? This question serves as a guiding contemplation for us as we proceed, inviting us to delve deeper into the significance of these twelve mental qualities and their role in the evolution from the Sons of Man to the Sons of God.

1. Reuben (Vision of Faith)

- Reuben embodies the aspect of seeing and discerning truth on a spiritual level. This vision is not merely physical sight but an inner perception that allows one to recognize spiritual truths beyond outer appearances. In the development of the spiritual mind, Reuben represents the first step of awareness—a form of faith that enables the soul to "see" or understand spiritual reality.

2. Simeon (Obedience and Receptivity)

- Simeon stands for the quality of hearing and obedience. This faculty is a mental attitude of receptivity, where the mind is open to divine guidance. The higher aspect of Simeon is an obedient and receptive state that allows the individual to be attuned to the voice of divine wisdom, developing a deeper understanding and readiness to act upon spiritual instruction.

3. Levi (Unity and Love)

- Levi represents the quality of unity, attachment, and love, which binds and connects. This faculty is not only about the physical bond but the spiritual union of the heart. In the mind of the "Son of Man," Levi is the force that brings together aspects of the self, creating harmony and strengthening the connection between the soul and its divine source.

4. Judah (Praise and Affirmation)

- Judah embodies the power of praise and affirmation, an active faculty that elevates the soul through acknowledgment of divine goodness. This quality is a foundational part of the mental structure, as it reinforces positivity and a higher consciousness. Through praise, Judah energizes and aligns the mind with the spiritual will, strengthening the soul's commitment to divine purpose.

5. Dan (Judgment and Discernment)

- Dan represents judgment and the ability to discern truth from falsehood. This faculty is critical for developing wisdom, as it empowers the individual to make sound decisions based on divine principles rather than mere appearances. Dan's discernment is necessary to maintain spiritual integrity, allowing one to navigate life with clarity and righteous judgment.

6. Naphtali (Strength and Resilience)

- Naphtali symbolizes strength and resilience, often associated with the inner vitality that sustains life's endeavors. This quality is a stabilizing force within the mind, enabling perseverance and the capacity to withstand challenges. In the spiritual mind, Naphtali upholds the energy and determination required to pursue higher goals.

7. Gad (Power and Command)

- Gad stands for the ability to assert power and take command. This quality is essential for manifesting divine will and expressing authority in alignment with spiritual principles. Gad's influence empowers the mind to be assertive, enabling the outward expression of inner convictions in service to truth and justice.

8. Asher (Joy and Blessing)

- Asher embodies joy, happiness, and the sense of blessing that comes from alignment with divine goodness. This faculty brings a sense of contentment and spiritual abundance, creating a harmonious and joyful state of mind. Asher is the quality that allows the soul to recognize and celebrate the blessings of spiritual life.

9. Issachar (Understanding and Reward)

- Issachar represents understanding and the reward of spiritual labor. This quality reflects the deep intellectual insight and comprehension of divine laws, leading to the realization of spiritual truths. In the mental structure of the "Son of Man," Issachar is the diligent seeker of wisdom, gaining rewards through persistent spiritual study and application.

10. Zebulun (Order and Stability)

- Zebulun is the quality of order, stability, and a sense of home or dwelling in the divine. This faculty maintains balance within the mind, ensuring that all aspects of the self are aligned and structured according to divine order. Zebulun's presence fosters a grounded approach to spirituality, providing a stable foundation for spiritual growth.

11. Joseph (Imagination and Increase)

- Joseph represents imagination, the capacity to envision divine ideas and bring them into form. This quality is expansive, symbolizing growth and the increasing manifestation of spiritual ideas in life. Joseph's role in the mind is one of creative vision and increase, continuously expanding the understanding and experience of divine truth.

Ephraim (Fruitfulness and Multiplication)

Ephraim signifies the aspect of fruitfulness and multiplication. This quality reflects the mind's ability to generate and bring forth new ideas, representing abundance in both thought and expression. Ephraim embodies the principle of expansion, the continuous unfolding and multiplication of divine ideas in life. It's a mental state that not only nurtures growth but also spreads the influence of these divine ideas throughout one's consciousness, multiplying blessings in all areas of life.

Manasseh (Memory and Forgetfulness)

Manasseh represents the faculty of memory, specifically the ability to let go of past limitations and grievances. This quality is a mental discipline of "forgetting" what no longer serves the soul's higher purpose, allowing the mind to remain focused on the present and future spiritual vision.

Manasseh embodies the spiritual principle of release, freeing the soul from attachments to past experiences that may hinder its progress. This mental quality helps one to remember divine origin while letting go of false identifications and unnecessary burdens.

12. Benjamin (Will and Determination)

- Benjamin stands for the strength of will and determination, the inner force that drives action. This faculty gives the individual the courage to pursue spiritual goals with unwavering resolve. In the spiritual mind, Benjamin ensures that the soul is steadfast, fully committed to realizing its divine purpose.

Interconnected Profiles: The Composite Mind of the "Son of Man"

The twelve qualities represented by each tribe form a unified mental structure within the "Son of Man." Together, they exemplify the full spectrum of spiritual faculties necessary for divine self-expression and realization. Each faculty, while distinct, is interdependent, reflecting the harmonious functioning of a higher consciousness.

1. **Faith (Reuben) and Discernment (Dan)** anchor the mind in spiritual perception and righteous judgment.
2. **Obedience (Simeon) and Receptivity (Levi)** cultivate an openness to divine instruction, unifying the mind in love and harmony.
3. **Praise (Judah)** amplifies the positive focus, while **Strength (Naphtali)** and **Command (Gad)** empower the mind to act with courage and authority.
4. **Joy (Asher) and Understanding (Issachar)** enrich the mind, bringing wisdom and contentment as fruits of spiritual alignment.
5. **Order (Zebulun)** provides stability, balancing the energies of **Imagination (Joseph)** and **Will (Benjamin)** to ensure a structured and purposeful manifestation of divine potential.

Through these faculties, the mind of the "Son of Man" achieves a state of completeness, embodying the full expression of divine qualities. Joseph's role, traditionally replaced by his sons Ephraim and Manasseh in the distribution of tribes, symbolizes the dual nature of the mental faculties—both as an expansive force (Ephraim) and as a reflective quality that aids in the recollection of divine purpose (Manasseh). This duality emphasizes that imagination (Joseph) functions both to create and to sustain spiritual remembrance, fulfilling the mind's capacity to grow and to remain aligned with divine origin.

In the upcoming lecture this metaphysical framework of the twelve tribes will serve as a foundation for understanding the twelve apostles, each representing an evolved expression of these mental faculties within the spiritual journey of the "Sons of God." This foundational structure demonstrates how the twelve qualities support spiritual evolution, preparing the mind to reflect divine attributes through conscious living.

Side Note:

Metaphysical Implications of Dan and Ephraim's Exclusion

In the Revelation narrative, the omission of Dan and Ephraim from the twelve tribes could signify a deeper metaphysical teaching. Each tribe represents an aspect of consciousness, and Revelation often illustrates the journey toward spiritual wholeness, or the "Christ within." The removal of certain tribes could thus be understood as symbolic of qualities or aspects that must be transcended or purified to reach this state of divine consciousness.

1. ***Dan****:* In the metaphysical profile, Dan represents judgment, discrimination, and discernment. While judgment is necessary in the lower stages of spiritual development, as it allows us to distinguish between truths and illusions, it can become a barrier when one aspires to divine consciousness. The Christ consciousness does not operate through the duality of judgment; rather, it embodies unconditional love and oneness. Therefore, the exclusion of Dan might suggest that as we ascend to this level, we must move beyond the limited, dualistic perspective of judgment. In this sense, leaving Dan out reflects the transcendence of judgment in favor of divine wisdom and pure perception.

2. ***Ephraim****:* Ephraim, associated with fruitfulness and the will, represents a fertile mind and the drive toward abundance and manifestation. While the will and creative fertility are essential qualities, they can be misaligned when driven by ego rather than spirit. Ephraim's exclusion might point to the idea that, in the pursuit of the Christ state, there is a need to surrender the personal will to the divine will. This surrender aligns our creative power with divine purpose rather than personal ambition. Thus, the omission of Ephraim highlights the importance of transcending personal desires to align fully with higher, divine intentions.

Unified Interpretation

The absence of Dan and Ephraim in the Revelation list symbolizes the need to move beyond judgment (Dan) and personal will (Ephraim) as we approach higher states of consciousness. Judgment limits us to seeing differences, creating a separation that contradicts the unity sought in divine consciousness. Similarly, personal will, when not aligned with divine intention, can tether us to egoistic desires, preventing full spiritual awakening. In the revelation of the Christ within, we are called to embody a transcendent state where judgment is replaced by divine wisdom and the personal will is surrendered to divine guidance. Dan and Ephraim's omission thus reflects the qualities that must be relinquished or refined as we seek the full embodiment of the Christ consciousness. This understanding reinforces that the journey to divine consciousness is one of purification and transcendence, shedding aspects that no longer serve as we ascend to our higher, unified self.

5th Entry

Prelude: The Path of the Twelve Apostles to the Christ Within

In the journey of spiritual awakening, the Twelve Apostles represent stages of consciousness, energies, and virtues that the soul encounters as it ascends from the earthly base to the divine crown. Each Apostle embodies a unique quality of the human spirit that must be integrated, transformed, or transcended to realize the Christ within. The path begins at the base, with Judas, the betrayer, and rises through layers of spiritual refinement until it reaches the divine revelation embodied in Jesus the Christ.

Apostles vs. Disciples: A Metaphysical Exploration

In our metaphysical journey, the distinction between "apostle" and "disciple" is profound, each representing different stages of spiritual evolution within the soul.

The Role of Disciples

The "disciples" symbolize the initial disciplined qualities within each person that are drawn to the spiritual ideal and guided by the Higher Self. These qualities, though still in a process of formation, possess the potential for higher realization. They are, in essence, seeds of divine attributes—faculties that aspire to the ideal but remain in the developmental phase, attached to the striving for inner harmony and guidance from the spiritual center.

The Transition to Apostles

The journey of these qualities culminates as they evolve into "apostles." Here, the disciple qualities have been refined, raised, and fully actualized into stable virtues that now serve as agents of divine expression.

The apostles are these qualities in their mature state, no longer merely followers but embodiments of higher wisdom and love. They represent the virtues now fully aligned with the central divine essence within, often depicted as the Christ consciousness.

The Spiritual Constellation of Apostles

Through the apostles, the divine spark within the soul is no longer an abstract potential but a radiating reality, each virtue in perfect alignment with the cosmic order. The twelve apostles thus form a spiritual constellation around the indwelling Christ, reflecting the perfected qualities nearest to the divine source within. They are akin to spiritual archetypes, personified virtues that are now firmly established and capable of guiding and uplifting the soul's lower aspects. In this context, apostles are not just messengers of divine truth but embodiments of it, infused with the power to instruct, heal, and transform.

The Calling of Disciples

Each disciple represents a quality still in the making, striving toward divine unity. The calling of a disciple is an invitation from the Spirit within, urging these qualities to rise to a higher purpose. When Jesus called his twelve disciples, he summoned these nascent virtues to take on their sacred role in service to the soul's evolution. This reflects the process by which the Higher Self guides these developing qualities to reach their highest expression.

The Transformation into Apostleship

As these qualities mature and align themselves with divine purpose, they are transmuted into apostles—virtues that no longer serve only the individual soul but the greater cosmic order. The apostles are thus qualities that have transcended personal attachments and now embody universal truth, capable of participating in the divine work of guiding and uplifting others.

From Aspiration to Cosmic Service

The apostles, then, symbolize qualities that have moved from personal aspiration (discipleship) to cosmic service (apostleship), each representing an aspect of divine wisdom, courage, or compassion. The transformation from disciple to apostle is the journey from self-oriented growth to selfless service, each quality evolving from an individual pursuit to a universal expression.

Final Distinction

Thus, the distinction between disciple and apostle is one of degree and purpose: disciples represent the inner qualities in the process of refinement and alignment with the divine, while apostles are these qualities in their fully realized form, acting in harmony with the divine will and serving as channels for the Higher Self's expression in the world.

The Apostolic Chakra Guide:

1. Judas Iscariot – The Energy of Betrayal and the Shadow (Base Chakra)

Judas represents the primal force bound to earthly desires, attachment, and the shadow self. His betrayal is symbolic of the soul's initial entrapment in the ego, where it must confront the darker aspects of human nature. As the foundation of our spiritual journey, Judas teaches us about the importance of recognizing and transforming our shadow, so we may rise beyond betrayal and attachment.

2. Thomas – The Energy of Doubt and Inquiry (Sacral Chakra)

Thomas, often called the Doubter, reflects the restless mind that questions, probes, and seeks evidence. This stage represents the sacral chakra, where the soul wrestles with faith and skepticism. Doubt is not the enemy of truth but rather the precursor to it; Thomas's journey is one of moving from skepticism toward deeper understanding, a necessary step in developing discernment and true belief.

3. Matthew – The Energy of Transformation and Redemption (Solar Plexus Chakra)

Matthew, the tax collector, symbolizes the power of transformation. From a life steeped in materialism, he moves towards spiritual purpose. Aligned with the solar plexus, Matthew represents the soul's struggle with personal power and worldly ambition.

His path teaches the soul to transmute selfish desires into selfless service, finding strength through inner transformation and dedication to a higher calling.

4. Philip – The Energy of Openness and Receptivity (Heart Chakra)

Philip embodies openness to divine truth and the willingness to seek out and understand the mysteries of the spirit. As a symbol of the heart chakra, Philip represents the energy of acceptance, compassion, and unity. His path is one of expanding beyond intellectual understanding into a heartfelt embrace of the divine. Through Philip, we learn the importance of softening the heart and becoming receptive to higher wisdom.

5. Bartholomew (Nathanael) – The Energy of Purity and Truth (Throat Chakra)

Bartholomew, also known as Nathanael, signifies the virtue of honesty and purity of speech. Representing the throat chakra, he embodies the energy of truth and integrity, unmasking illusions. His path challenges the soul to speak and live in alignment with inner truth. Through Bartholomew, we learn that clear, sincere expression is the foundation of authentic communication with the divine.

6. James the Lesser – The Energy of Humility and Innocence (Third Eye Chakra)

James the Lesser represents humility, often working in the background, unseen. As a figure aligned with the third eye chakra, he teaches us that vision does not always come from prominence but from purity of intention and a quiet inner life. His path embodies the spiritual virtue of humility, encouraging us to let go of pride and ego. In doing so, we open ourselves to true insight and the hidden mysteries of the spirit.

7. Simon the Zealot – The Energy of Passion and Devotion (Crown Chakra Base)

Simon the Zealot embodies the fiery energy of zeal and spiritual fervor, the base of the crown chakra's transformative fire. His passion is a reflection of dedication and unwavering commitment to divine principles. As the soul reaches the threshold of transcendence, Simon teaches us that this journey demands total devotion. His energy purifies the soul's remaining attachments, preparing it for union with the divine.

8. James the Greater – The Energy of Inner Strength and Witnessing (Crown Chakra Opening)

James the Greater symbolizes the strength to stand as a witness to the truth, no matter the personal cost. Positioned at the opening of the crown, he represents steadfastness and the courage to live by divine principles. His energy teaches the soul to embody divine truth as a lived reality, standing firm and unshakeable in the face of adversity.

9. John – The Energy of Love and Mystical Vision (Higher Crown)

John, the Beloved, is the Apostle of love and mystical vision, representing the higher crown energies. Through his intimate relationship with Jesus, John embodies the soul's purest desire for union with the divine. His path teaches us about the profound power of love as the bridge to higher wisdom and the mysteries of the soul. John opens the way to Christ consciousness through love's limitless depth.

10. Andrew – The Energy of Faith and Introduction (Christ Consciousness Awakening)

Andrew, the one who brought others to Jesus, signifies the energy of faith and connection. In the awakening of Christ consciousness, Andrew represents the willingness to introduce, to reach out, and to bring others into the fold of divine awareness. His path reminds the soul of the importance of sharing faith, a step that awakens the Christ potential within and reinforces unity.

11. Peter – The Energy of Foundation and Faithfulness (Christ Consciousness Grounding)

Peter, the rock upon which Jesus built his church, represents the grounding force of faith that supports the soul's divine potential. As the soul prepares for the full revelation of the Christ within, Peter embodies the stability and strength necessary to hold this consciousness. His journey shows us that faith is the bedrock of the spiritual path and that enduring commitment allows us to fully embody Christ consciousness.

12. Thaddeus (Jude) – The Energy of Revelation and Guidance (Higher Crown Opening)

Jude, often known as the bringer of hope and revelation, stands at the higher crown, offering guidance and insight. His path represents the opening of divine revelation, a reminder that the soul, at this level of consciousness, must trust in divine guidance. Jude's energy is one of communion, illuminating the path toward union with the Christ within.

The Christ – The Crown of Revelation and Unity

Through the path of these Twelve Apostles, the soul ascends from earthly desires and attachments, passing through the layers of transformation, truth, humility, passion, and love. Each Apostle represents a step toward spiritual maturity, an energy that must be integrated and transcended. The culmination of this journey is the Christ consciousness, the revelation of the divine within, the light that illuminates the crown. Jesus the Christ is not merely the destination but the ultimate reflection of our true nature. He is the awakened self, the eternal light that reveals the soul's inherent unity with God.

In this journey, the Christ within awakens as the fullness of divine love, wisdom, and compassion. It is the ultimate realization that all energies, all apostles, and all paths converge in this supreme truth—the Christ within is the Son of God, the eternal and undivided light that resides at the very center of our being.

This prelude prepares us for the deeper exploration of Jesus the Christ, the embodiment of divine consciousness, whose life and teachings are the blueprint for our own spiritual journey. As we move forward into the lecture, we step into the wisdom of the Christ, embracing the path of self-realization and union with the divine.

Judas: *The Alchemy of Betrayal - Redeeming the Judas within the Suns of God.*

Welcome, Sons of God, to another chapter in our exploration of the deeper metaphysical profiles of figures who serve as both archetypes and reflections of our own journey towards self-realization. Today, we turn our focus to the Apostle Judas Iscariot—a figure who, at first glance, appears to symbolize betrayal, but who holds within his story a profound, transformative power that can guide us through the darker regions of our spiritual path.

In this lecture, we will go beyond the traditional narrative of Judas. We will explore him not merely as a disciple who betrayed Christ, but as an embodiment of the lower faculties within ourselves—the aspects of consciousness that must be confronted, understood, and ultimately transmuted on the path to enlightenment. Judas is a mirror, a symbolic reflection of the inner challenges that each of us must face to reach spiritual maturity. His story invites us to delve into the shadow within, to walk through the "night of the soul" where our own lower tendencies are laid bare. And through his journey, we come to see that every fall, every limitation, every descent into darkness is, in truth, a vital step toward the light.

As we move through this lecture, I invite you to set aside preconceived notions and consider Judas as a necessary aspect of the journey—the part of ourselves that must first stumble before it can rise. We will examine how his actions, while seemingly condemnable on the surface, contain essential lessons for the Sons of God.

We will see that Judas, far from being an outcast in our inner pantheon, is instead a catalyst for transformation, urging us to release our grip on ego-driven desires and to open ourselves fully to divine love.

With this introduction, let us begin our journey into the metaphysical profile of Judas Iscariot and discover how, in recognizing and redeeming the Judas within, we are drawn closer to our divine essence.

Judas as the Catalyst for Self-Realization

Judas Iscariot holds a unique role in the spiritual landscape of the soul's evolution, a role that goes beyond his historical narrative. Today, we will journey into the depths of his symbolic meaning and discover how, rather than being a mere antagonist, Judas represents the inner forces that catalyze our transformation.

First, let us understand Judas as **the catalyst for self-realization**. He represents the raw, unenlightened elements within our consciousness—the forces of desire, greed, and self-centeredness that often lead us into conflict and suffering. Yet, these qualities are not to be rejected outright. They are part of our spiritual anatomy, necessary for the journey of evolution. Through Judas, we see a part of ourselves that must confront the temptation of materialism, the desire to control, and the clinging to egoic identities. These are the shadows we must face within, and it is only by grappling with these aspects that we can come to understand and, ultimately, transcend them.

In a metaphysical sense, Judas's betrayal is not simply an outward act of disloyalty; it is an internal confrontation with the limitations of our own ego. He embodies the duality within us—our capacity for ignorance as well as our potential for enlightenment. In this way, he serves as a guide through our own limitations, pushing us to question, to challenge, and to go beyond the small self.

The Judas Archetype as the Journey Through Darkness

Moving deeper, we encounter **the Judas archetype as the journey through darkness**. This darkness is the soul's night, a stage in which ignorance, doubt, and fear emerge, testing the very core of our faith and resilience. Sons of God, as you walk your path to higher consciousness, you will encounter your own inner Judas—a part of you that succumbs to lower impulses, that momentarily loses sight of the divine within. This is an essential phase, one where the soul is both tested and refined. It is through the experience of limitation, just as Saturn represents in the cosmos, that we come to the precipice of transformation. Saturn, like Judas, brings us to the edge of our physical and mental limits, forcing us to confront our attachments and fears. And it is through this confrontation that we are readied for the rebirth of higher consciousness.

Transformation and Redemption: The Ultimate Role of Judas

Now we come to the heart of Judas's role: **transformation and redemption**. Despite the darkness he embodies, Judas holds the potential for ultimate redemption. He represents the human capacity to fall, yet also the capacity to rise through inner transformation. When we view Judas through the lens of metaphysics, we see that his acquisitive nature—his desire to possess and control—mirrors the part of us that seeks material and egoic fulfillment. But in its purified form, this faculty becomes one of spiritual gratitude and praise. The redeemed Judas is no longer grasping but is instead filled with thanksgiving for divine abundance. This is the path of transformation, where each Sons of God learns to transmute their lower desires into spiritual nourishment.

In this process, we see that Judas is not to be condemned but rather understood as an instrument of divine purpose. Recognizing our inner Judas is not an act of rejection but of integration. In embracing this part of ourselves, we initiate the process of redemption—where ego-driven desires are surrendered, and divine love begins to permeate our consciousness.

Love and the Final Transmutation of the Judas Faculty

At the highest level of this journey, **love becomes the transformative force that redeems the Judas within**. Love is the force that dissolves the ego's need to possess, that overcomes the fear-driven impulses of the lower self. For the Sons of God, love is not merely a sentiment but an alchemical process that reshapes the soul, turning selfishness into selflessness.

It is through love that Judas, once the figure of betrayal, becomes Judah—the faculty of spiritual appropriation, no longer seeking to own but to give in union with the divine will.

This transmutation is the goal of the spiritual journey. When we fully surrender our ego, allowing divine love to flow through every action and thought, Judas becomes a beacon of divine purpose within us. He transforms from a shadowy figure of betrayal to a symbol of redeemed humanity, reminding us that even our darkest aspects can serve as steps toward enlightenment.

Side Note:

In the metaphysical understanding, ***Judas Iscariot*** represents the acquisitive aspect of consciousness, particularly the attachment to material gains and lower desires that often lead one astray from the higher path. Judas symbolizes the part of the self that can betray divine intention by succumbing to earthly inclinations.

His actions reveal the potential pitfalls when one's focus remains anchored in the physical realm rather than in spiritual growth.

Matthias, chosen to replace **Judas**, represents the conscious transformation and uplifting of this acquisitive faculty. **Matthias** embodies the *"gift of Jehovah"* or the process of dedicating this life energy wholly to divine purpose. This transition from Judas to **Matthias** signifies the redirection of one's acquisitive faculties toward spiritual aims, enabling the individual to "lay hold" of higher attainments. Through this conscious redirection, the very faculty that once led to betrayal now aids in achieving eternal life and aligning with the indwelling Christ consciousness, symbolizing divine I AM presence.

In essence, **Matthias's** entry into the discipleship reflects the opportunity for redemption and spiritual ascension that lies within all aspects of the self, even those that may have once strayed from the path. By transforming this faculty from material attachment to spiritual devotion, the individual achieves a more complete alignment with divine purpose, reinforcing the idea that every part of our consciousness can be reclaimed and repurposed for spiritual evolution.

Conclusion: Embracing the Shadow: Judas as a Pathway to Divine Union

Sons of God, as we conclude this lecture, remember that the story of Judas is not one of condemnation but of transformation. By recognizing and redeeming the Judas within, you are not defeated by your lower tendencies but empowered to transform them.

This is the essence of the spiritual journey—to integrate every part of the self, even the parts we may wish to deny or ignore.

Judas, then, is not an outcast but a necessary catalyst on the path to union with the divine. Through him, we learn that every limitation, every fall, and every moment of ignorance holds within it the seed of awakening. His journey from darkness to light is our journey, and his redemption is our ultimate goal. In embracing Judas, we embrace the totality of our being, moving ever closer to the divine within.

Thus, Judas becomes not a figure to be despised, but a profound aspect of the self to be understood and transformed. In his story, we see the eternal path from limitation to liberation, from separation to unity with the divine.

Thomas (Didymus): *Alchemy of Doubt - The Twin Flame of Reason and Revelation*

Introduction to Thomas, the Doubting Disciple

In our journey through the metaphysical dimensions of the Apostles, we now turn to Thomas, also known as Didymus, which signifies "twin" or "double." Thomas, within the framework of the soul's faculties, embodies the principles of reason and intellectual discernment. His presence among the Apostles is not merely symbolic of skepticism but an archetype for the mind's quest to understand and verify truth. This "twin" nature speaks to the duality inherent in human perception—the split between faith and reason, spiritual insight and intellectual inquiry. Thomas represents the analytical mind's necessity to witness, test, and confirm reality, challenging the soul to bridge the gap between sensory evidence and spiritual truth.

Thomas and the Role of Intellectual Perception

Thomas' request for tangible proof of Christ's resurrection illuminates his role as the faculty of intellectual truth-seeking within the collective spiritual organism of the Sons of God. Unlike the blind faith often attributed to other Apostles, Thomas requires experiential knowledge. This trait aligns with a deeper metaphysical principle: the journey from perception to inner knowing.

Intellectual perception, as personified by Thomas, encourages the Sons of God to transcend mere belief, to transform doubt into a profound, unshakeable understanding grounded in experiential reality.

This desire for proof, while seemingly an obstacle, is in fact an essential stage in spiritual evolution. It signifies the disciplined mind's journey from reliance on external validation to the realization of inner divinity. Thomas' doubt, therefore, is not a weakness but a necessary function that sharpens the mind, enabling it to transcend its limitations and achieve unity with the higher self.

Understanding as the Gateway to the "I AM"

Thomas' quest for verification also reflects his symbolic alignment with the head, the seat of intellectual reasoning. In John 14:5, Thomas's question draws forth Christ's declaration: "I am the way, the truth, and the life." This statement signifies that the path to divine understanding is through the "I AM" presence within, an inner gateway that the Sons of God must recognize as the entry point to the kingdom of God. For Thomas, and by extension the Sons of God, understanding begins with questioning, but culminates in an inward journey that reveals the "I AM" as the ultimate reality.

Thus, Thomas' nature teaches us that true understanding transcends mere intellectual knowledge; it is the realization of the Christ within, the divine "I AM" that serves as both guide and destination.

This aspect of Thomas as the questioning mind reflects the divine mandate to discern, test, and ultimately transcend intellectual limitations through a profound inner experience of divine truth.

The Twin Nature and the Principle of Duality

The concept of Thomas as "Didymus," the twin, holds a layered metaphysical significance. This duality speaks to the relationship between the higher and lower selves—the spiritual and the intellectual facets within each Son of God. The twin nature of Thomas suggests that the path of intellectual discernment is inherently double-edged, requiring a balance between the outer mind and the inner spirit. In this dynamic, Thomas exemplifies the process by which intellect must eventually yield to inner wisdom, acknowledging its limitations and embracing the unity of spiritual truth beyond duality.

This twinship symbolizes the union of complementary aspects within the individual: intellect with intuition, reason with faith, and knowledge with wisdom. In embodying this duality, Thomas teaches that the Sons of God must reconcile these polarities, embracing their intellectual faculties while remaining open to the mysteries beyond comprehension.

This journey toward reconciliation is a microcosm of the greater spiritual alchemy that unites the fragmented aspects of the self into wholeness.

Transcending Doubt: From Skepticism to Spiritual Certainty

Thomas' initial skepticism about Christ's resurrection is a reminder that doubt serves as the crucible in which true faith is forged. For the Sons of God, doubt is not a barrier but a gateway; it is the catalyst that propels the soul from mere acceptance to experiential certainty. In this sense, Thomas represents the critical function of discernment, which purifies and elevates faith, transforming it from blind acceptance to conscious, awakened knowledge.

As the Sons of God journey through phases of questioning and uncertainty, they engage in a sacred alchemical process, refining their understanding and aligning their intellect with spiritual truth. Thomas' insistence on physical proof illustrates the soul's yearning to know, rather than simply to believe. Through this process, doubt becomes a transformative force, guiding the intellect to a higher state of knowing—a knowing that is experiential, lived, and realized within.

Applying Thomas' Metaphysical Archetype in Daily Practice

The metaphysical profile of Thomas, as both the doubter and the seeker of truth, challenges the Sons of God to examine their own reliance on external validation. Thomas' journey invites us to practice discernment, to honor the questions that arise within, and to pursue a path of intellectual integrity.

This is not a rejection of faith, but a call to deepen it through conscious inquiry, bridging the mind's understanding with the heart's wisdom.

To embody the spirit of Thomas is to recognize that true faith is an inner knowing that emerges from experiential encounters with truth. The Sons of God are thus called to integrate Thomas' qualities within themselves, to honor doubt as a tool of growth, and to strive for a balance between reason and spiritual insight.

In doing so, they transform intellectual perception into a faculty aligned with divine wisdom, elevating the mind to its rightful place as a servant of the higher self.

Conclusion: Thomas as the Metaphysical Mirror

In the metaphysical framework, Thomas serves as a mirror for the Sons of God, reflecting the inner journey of intellectual discernment. His journey from doubt to understanding exemplifies the sacred role of reason in the soul's evolution. By embracing Thomas' archetype, the Sons of God learn that true understanding is not found in blind acceptance but in the alchemical marriage of intellect and intuition. Through this balance, they are guided toward the realization that the ultimate truth—the divine "I AM"—lies not in external proofs but within the sanctified chambers of the soul.

In closing, let Thomas stand as a reminder that doubt, when embraced as part of the spiritual path, becomes a powerful force for awakening. For in the embrace of both certainty and uncertainty, the Sons of God discover the fullness of divine truth, uniting the twin aspects of the self into a harmonious whole, where intellect serves the wisdom of the spirit and leads each seeker to the light of inner realization.

Matthew (Levi) *as the Archetype of Divine Will Discipleship, Surrender, and Spiritual Realization*

Introduction Welcome, Sons of God. Today, we will examine the metaphysical qualities embodied by the Apostle Matthew, also known as Levi. Matthew's life as a tax collector turned disciple reveals profound insights about the nature of will, transformation, and the relinquishment of worldly attachments in pursuit of higher consciousness. Through his story, we see the journey of aligning personal will with divine will, a journey each of you is called to undertake.

In this lecture, we will explore Matthew's role as the will faculty within the soul, his transformation from material attachment to spiritual dedication, and the symbolic meanings behind his connections to the name Levi and his role as a follower of Christ.

Matthew as the Embodiment of the Will

Matthew represents the will faculty in the human soul—the power to decide, direct, and commit. In the human body, this faculty is often associated with the forehead, the place of focused intent and purpose. The will, as a disciplined force, shapes one's path, influencing decisions that steer life's direction. However, for the Sons of God, this will must transcend mere personal ambition and align with a higher purpose.

In his former life as a tax collector, Matthew was bound by the pursuits of wealth and accumulation, externalizing his will through material gain. This external orientation is common for many, as they seek validation, security, and power through worldly possessions. But, as Matthew demonstrates, true will must be directed inward, toward the development of spiritual integrity and alignment with divine purpose.

Deeper Insight

The transformation Matthew undergoes symbolizes the turning of the will from external desires to internal dedication. This shift is not merely a decision but a deep, continuous commitment to renounce lesser inclinations for a higher ideal. Matthew teaches us that the path of spiritual awakening involves the disciplined conversion of our desires and attachments into a force that serves the divine.

The Significance of Levi and Spiritual Transformation

Matthew's name, Levi, connects him symbolically to the priestly tribe of Israel, tasked with the sacred duty of serving and teaching the law of God. In a metaphysical context, Levi represents the faculty of love, as love in divine consciousness is the cohesive force that unites all aspects of the soul. When love is expressed through the will, it elevates desire from mere personal gain to the pursuit of spiritual enlightenment and service.

As Levi, Matthew's role reflects the uniting power of love, which draws all faculties of the mind toward harmony with divine truth. The shift from Levi to Matthew, or from love-centered unity to a will-aligned purpose, exemplifies the spiritual journey of balancing love and will. This transformation is essential for the Sons of God, as it illustrates how disciplined will must be informed by love to serve a purpose greater than itself.

Deeper Insight

In relinquishing his attachment to wealth and embracing his role as a disciple, Matthew demonstrates the power of consecrated will—a will that is wholly devoted to divine service. This dedication is what makes one's will an instrument of higher power. Through Matthew, we learn that when the will is infused with love, it becomes capable of transcending ego-driven desires and aligning with the eternal principles of divine order.

The Calling of Matthew – Will in Service of Divine Guidance

When Jesus calls Matthew to leave his occupation and follow him, it symbolizes the call each soul receives to transcend its attachments to the material world and align itself with divine purpose. This calling is not limited to Matthew; it resonates with the spiritual journey each of you is on. Answering the call requires not only a shift in actions but a fundamental transformation of intent—redirecting one's focus from self-serving goals to the embodiment of divine will.

In answering this call, Matthew demonstrates the surrender of personal ambition for spiritual obedience. This act of surrender is one of the highest expressions of will, as it involves the conscious choice to align personal desires with divine intention. Through prayer, meditation, and disciplined focus, the will is refined and becomes receptive to higher guidance.

Deeper Insight

Matthew's story teaches that the will must be disciplined, yet receptive. It must be resolute in its purpose but open to the subtle promptings of the Spirit. For the Sons of God, this means cultivating a will that is neither rigid nor overly flexible but balanced in its strength and sensitivity. Only then can the will act as an instrument of divine intention, manifesting the higher purpose within the material world.

The Apostolic Will and the Path of Regeneration

The transition from a life of accumulation to one of discipleship mirrors the process of regeneration. Regeneration, in this context, is the gradual transformation of all faculties of the mind, as they are disciplined and brought into harmony with divine order. In this journey, Matthew exemplifies the essential role of will, as it directs, disciplines, and harmonizes the inner faculties of the soul.

The spiritual journey requires a will that is both guiding and governed. As Matthew's story illustrates, the will must not impose itself on external circumstances but rather govern the inner faculties, ensuring that they function in harmony. This inner alignment leads to outer transformation, as the will, guided by divine principles, reorders the mind and spirit.

Deeper Insight

For the Sons of God, Matthew's role serves as a reminder that regeneration begins within. The will must be devoted to internal mastery before it can influence external realities. This devotion involves an unyielding commitment to truth, the humility to surrender to divine guidance, and the courage to forsake attachments that no longer serve the soul's evolution.

The Metaphysical Significance of Discipleship

Discipleship, as seen in Matthew's life, represents the highest form of disciplined will. Each of the twelve apostles signifies a faculty or quality that, when disciplined, becomes capable of receiving higher teaching and embodying divine truth. Matthew, as the will, serves as the anchor for these qualities, ensuring that they function in alignment with the Christ within.

To be a disciple is to be a student of divine wisdom, a seeker of truth, and a vessel for spiritual realization. It is through the discipline of will that one adheres to the path, overcoming distractions and staying attuned to the inner guidance of the

Spirit. For the Sons of God, discipleship calls for a dedicated will that is unwavering in its pursuit of divine alignment.

Deeper Insight

In surrendering to discipleship, the Sons of God are not merely following a teacher; they are embodying the principles of divine order within themselves. Matthew's journey from tax collector to disciple exemplifies this path of self-mastery and dedication. The Sons of God must cultivate a will that is both receptive to higher wisdom and committed to embodying that wisdom in every aspect of life.

Anchoring the Divine Will: Final Reflections on Matthew's Spiritual Pathway

In closing, Matthew, as the embodiment of divine will, calls each of you to awaken this faculty within yourselves. His journey from worldly pursuits to spiritual dedication teaches that the will, when aligned with love and informed by divine guidance, becomes a force for transformation, both within and without. As Sons of God, you are called to cultivate a will that is not driven by external desires but rooted in spiritual principles.

This will, disciplined and dedicated, becomes the foundation upon which the soul's higher faculties can flourish. Through Matthew, we learn that true discipleship involves the surrender of personal ambition, the cultivation of inner discipline, and the unwavering commitment to align with the divine purpose. May you, like Matthew, embrace this path of alignment, allowing the will to serve as a bridge between the divine mind and manifest reality.

Philip: *Courage, Power, and the Voice as Manifestation*

Welcome, Sons of God. Today, we embark on an exploration of the metaphysical essence of the Apostle Philip, delving into the qualities of courage, power, and the voice as a manifestation of spiritual authority. Philip the Apostle is not just a historical figure; he is a symbol, a profound archetype representing aspects of the soul that you are called to embody and awaken.

Philip's very name, "lover of horses," holds rich symbolism. Just as a skilled rider must harness the powerful energy of a spirited horse, so too does Philip teach you to command and direct your own inner forces. His qualities of courage and power are not limited to physical expression; they embody a resonant, spiritual force—a foundation for the development of higher consciousness.

The Principle of Inner Courage and Calculative Power

First, let us examine the principle of courage intertwined with calculative power. Philip's courage is not mere bravado or reckless action. It is a refined, measured force—a will to truth that weighs, estimates, and navigates. For you, the Sons of God, this principle emerges as an inner strength, enabling you to confront both internal and external forces that may attempt to deter you from the spiritual path.

In Philip, you witness the harmony between courage and intellectual discernment. This teaches that true courage is not blind bravery, but one that incorporates wisdom and foresight. As you awaken Philip's presence within, you balance raw courage with discernment, understanding that every decision and action should serve the path to divine truth.

Philip as the Gatekeeper of the Spiritual Word

Through Philip, you gain insights into the significance of the spoken word. In metaphysical terms, the throat represents the power center, the gateway where your inner life is manifested into the external world. Philip personifies the disciplined word—speech that is charged with divine intention, carrying the transformative potential of life itself.

When you speak from this center, your words resonate with a unique spiritual authority, creating waves of transformation and enlightenment. The spoken word, when infused with 'soul contact,' transcends mundane speech; it becomes an expression of your inner divinity. Christ's words are described as "spirit and life," reminding you of the transformative power that lies within a fully awakened, aligned voice.

The Role of Power in Spiritual Mastery

Next, consider Philip's embodiment of power, which is not about external dominance but about inner mastery. Philip serves as a symbol of spiritual dominion where primal desires and ego-driven impulses are subdued under the soul's authority. This is the essence of true power for you, Sons of God—the recognition that mastery begins within.

For the initiated, the voice becomes both an expression of spiritual depth and a tool for inner alchemy. By mastering the throat center, you learn to project higher vibrational energies, influencing your personal realms and harmonizing with the greater cosmic symphony. Philip's power teaches that true authority comes not from exertion over others but through self-discipline and alignment with divine will.

Philip and the Twelve Disciplined Qualities of the Soul

Philip's metaphysical profile is deeply tied to the twelve disciplined qualities of the soul. Each Apostle represents an aspect of divine consciousness, harmonized under the Higher Self, or the Christ within. Philip stands as courage and calculative capacity, a reminder to you that fortitude and wisdom must walk hand in hand.

In the context of the Twelve Apostles, Philip's presence reinforces the idea that these qualities work in unity, each one an avenue for divine energy to express itself. Together, they form a vessel for the indwelling Christ. You are encouraged to view the Twelve Apostles as twelve facets of the soul, each supporting the others, bringing balance and wholeness to your journey of spiritual awakening.

Metaphysical Implications for the Sons of God

As you delve into Philip's qualities, you find a profound reminder of the spiritual responsibilities associated with controlled speech, clear intention, and courageous action. Philip teaches you that every word and action should serve a higher purpose. In embodying Philip, you commit yourself to a disciplined path where each spoken word is a channel for divine intent, a force of spiritual transformation in the world.

This is your call not only to follow divine truth but to actively manifest it. As Sons of God, you recognize that courage, wisdom, and spiritual responsibility are the hallmarks of the initiated soul. Through Philip, you learn to wield these qualities in service to the highest good, allowing you to become instruments of divine power.

The Final Ascension: Voice as Eternal Expression

Finally, consider Philip's journey towards the ultimate realization—the voice as eternal expression. When you speak from a place of divine truth, that resonance is woven into the fabric of creation. As it is written, "Heaven and earth may pass away, but my words shall not pass away." This is the legacy of Philip—a voice that transcends mortality, a voice that continues to echo in eternity.

In this final act, find your voices not as instruments of personal will, but as vessels for the Eternal Word. When your voice is aligned with the divine, it becomes an instrument of healing, transformation, and alignment with the timeless.

Conclusion: Stepping into Divine Authority

In conclusion, this exploration of Philip's metaphysical attributes serves as a guiding light for you, the Sons of God, encouraging you to embody the courage, discipline, and spiritual authority that Philip represents. Each aspect of Philip is an inner quality awaiting recognition and awakening. Through Philip's profile, you are reminded that the journey to divinity requires disciplined courage, harmonious speech, and steadfast alignment with the Higher Self. May you carry these lessons within, striving to be true beacons of light and wisdom along the path of enlightenment.

Bartholomew (Nathanael): *Imagination and Divine Vision for the Sons of God*

We gather here, Sons of God, to delve into the spiritual essence of Bartholomew, also known as Nathanael. Bartholomew's presence in the apostolic circle is both profound and mysterious, his essence concealed within the folds of scripture. His role speaks to a facet of spiritual life that is essential, yet often veiled: the power of divine imagination. This is not the simple imagination that constructs illusions or flights of fancy, but rather the potent imaginative faculty that acts as a bridge between higher realms of consciousness and manifest reality. In this session, we will unravel the layers of Bartholomew's significance, his associations with Philip, Mark, and Luke, and the metaphysical implications these connections bring.

Bartholomew as Divine Imagination

In the metaphysical understanding, Bartholomew represents the faculty of divine imagination, the aspect within each of us that is capable of envisioning beyond the material and perceiving the profound possibilities held within the divine mind. Imagination, in this context, is not mere fantasy—it is the active, disciplined envisioning of the divine will and truth that shapes our reality. When this imagination is refined, it aligns with divine consciousness, enabling one to glimpse the sacred patterns underlying all existence.

Deeper Insight: Imagination, as represented by Bartholomew, becomes a sacred tool when attuned to divine principles. This is the imagination that allows the Sons of God to access the "blueprints" of higher wisdom. Bartholomew's relative obscurity in the Gospels reflects the hidden, inner work required to cultivate this faculty, as true imagination requires both purity and subtlety. It is a visionary power that, when activated, reveals the intrinsic unity between the human soul and divine intention. Thus, the Sons of God are called not merely to imagine but to imagine divinely, developing a consciousness that perceives and channels divine order into earthly form.

This imagination, however, requires refinement and discipline. Bartholomew's relative obscurity in the Gospels reflects the hidden, inner work required to cultivate this faculty. The imagination capable of manifesting divine vision is delicate and elusive, requiring deep introspection, unwavering focus, and spiritual attunement. Bartholomew teaches the Sons of God that this sacred imagination is foundational for spiritual evolution—it is the seedbed of all transformative visions.

The Significance of Nathanael and His Connection to Philip

In the Gospel of John, Nathanael's connection with Philip is highlighted. This association is not coincidental but is imbued with profound metaphysical significance. Philip, in metaphysical terms, represents the power of active faith and inquiry—a necessary force for awakening imagination.

Faith acts as the grounding force that stabilizes the lofty visions of the imagination, ensuring that these divine insights are brought into reality with strength and clarity.

Nathanael's initial skepticism—"Can anything good come out of Nazareth?"—reflects a hesitation within the mind, often bound by doubt, to fully trust in the expansive power of imagination. In this context, Nazareth signifies the journey of spiritual refinement, representing a place within the soul where transformation and growth toward higher truths occur. By questioning the potential of such a transformative journey, Nathanael's doubt reveals a reluctance to believe in the soul's capacity for spiritual evolution.

When Philip invites Nathanael to meet Jesus, an essential inner movement takes place. Philip, embodying faith as an active and encouraging force, represents the aspect of the self that nudges imagination to transcend its limitations and aspire toward divine understanding. In this interaction, Philip becomes the bridge between belief and imagination, prompting an inner alignment where faith elevates the imagination to a place where it can perceive the sacred.

Upon encountering Jesus, who represents the awakened divine presence within, Nathanael recognizes truth and exclaims, "Rabbi, you are the Son of God." This shift in perspective is profound; it signifies the moment when imagination, freed from doubt and guided by faith, achieves the vision to perceive the divine.

For those on a spiritual journey, this interaction teaches that the power of imagination, when rooted in unwavering trust, becomes a pathway to recognize and align with higher spiritual truths. This process is not merely a rational journey but an awakening of the inner faculties, where faith and imagination harmonize, allowing the soul to glimpse its divine nature.

For the Sons of God, this interplay between Nathanael and Philip serves as a reminder that imagination must be bolstered by faith. Without faith, imagination may wander or falter; with faith, it becomes a conduit for divine insight.

The Triad of Bartholomew, Mark, and Luke—Imagination, Transformation, and Wisdom

Bartholomew is frequently linked with Mark and Luke, and this triad carries immense metaphysical implications. Mark embodies transformation through action and courage, while Luke represents wisdom and intellectual discernment. Together with Bartholomew's imagination, they form a trinity of faculties essential for spiritual mastery.

Mark as Transformation: Mark's narrative often focuses on immediacy and decisive action. In metaphysical terms, Mark reflects the courage needed to act upon divine visions. Bartholomew's imagination must align with Mark's transformative courage to manifest in the material world.

When imagination is coupled with action, the Sons of God can create real change, moving divine ideas from potentiality into reality. This synthesis teaches that imagination, without the will to act, remains unfulfilled.

Luke as Wisdom: Luke, the physician and writer, embodies intellectual insight and wisdom. He represents the balanced application of knowledge that grounds imagination in truth. Imagination, when detached from wisdom, can lead to illusion. Luke's presence in the triad reminds us that wisdom is the guiding principle that harmonizes the faculties, ensuring that imagination serves the higher good rather than personal fantasy.

For the Sons of God, the interaction between Bartholomew, Mark, and Luke serves as a blueprint for inner alchemy. Divine imagination (Bartholomew), when united with the courage to act (Mark) and grounded in wisdom (Luke), becomes a force capable of transcending the limitations of the material world and manifesting divine purpose.

The Conflict Between Mark, Paul, and Barnabas —Metaphysical Implications

In Acts, we witness a disagreement between Paul and Barnabas regarding Mark, a conflict that is not merely historical but holds a deep metaphysical lesson. Paul represents the will aligned with truth and conviction, while Barnabas symbolizes encouragement and support.

Their dispute over Mark reflects the inner tension that often arises between discipline and flexibility within spiritual growth.

Deeper Insight: This conflict symbolizes the necessary balance between discipline and nurturing within the development of imagination. Paul's reluctance to bring Mark reflects the rigor and discernment required to channel imagination effectively, while Barnabas's support emphasizes the role of compassion in nurturing this faculty. The Sons of God are reminded that while discipline sharpens imagination, compassion allows it to grow. Both forces must work in harmony to cultivate an imagination that is powerful yet grounded in love and wisdom.

Mark's role in this scenario highlights the challenges imagination faces when transitioning into action. Paul's reluctance to bring Mark reflects the discipline required to hone imagination, while Barnabas's defense of Mark emphasizes the compassion and encouragement necessary to nurture this faculty. For the Sons of God, this dynamic teaches that imagination must be tempered by both discipline and compassion to reach its fullest expression.

Conclusion: Awakening the Divine Imagination

For the Sons of God, the faculty of imagination as embodied by Bartholomew/Nathanael is a divine inheritance that must be awakened, disciplined, and directed. Imagination, when fully aligned with truth, faith, courage, and compassion, becomes a tool for spiritual creation and a means of realizing the divine kingdom within. By understanding and embodying the metaphysical profiles of Bartholomew, Philip, Mark, and Luke, the Sons of God are called to harness their imagination as a force for transformation, both within themselves and within the world.

As we close this lecture, let us contemplate the fig tree of Nathanael—the inner place of quiet vision—and remember that divine imagination is both a privilege and a responsibility. It is a gift that enables us to see beyond appearances, to envision a higher reality, and to serve as co-creators with the Divine. May each Son of God nurture this faculty with the highest reverence, understanding that through imagination, we touch the very mind of God, bringing forth light and wisdom into the world.

Side Note: In metaphysical symbolism, the name *"Nathaniel,"* particularly with its suffix **"EL**," which means "of God" or "God," suggests a deep connection to divine qualities. "Nathani**el**" translates to "Gift of God" or "Given by God," emphasizing a bestowed quality or blessing that comes directly from the Divine source. In this sense, Nathani**el**, or Bartholomew, represents the "gift" of divinely inspired perception or insight, aligning with the mystical faculty of intuition. This "gift of God" is akin to a direct line to divine understanding, one that is less filtered by reason or intellect alone and more aligned with pure, intuitive knowing. Bartholomew, as Nathani**el**, thus symbolizes a purity of inner sight or perception—an ability to see beyond the material and discern the divine essence within all things, reflecting a spiritual clarity aligned with higher truths.

By incorporating **"EL"** in his name, Nathani**el** also resonates with the divine attributes of light and truth, anchoring his spiritual role within the framework of the Twelve Apostles as one who brings the gift of divine insight, not only for himself but also as an inspiration for others. This name, therefore, links Bartholomew/Nathani**el**'s role to the function of divine wisdom, insight, and clarity in the spiritual journey, making him an embodiment of divine perception within the metaphysical profiles.

James: *The Metaphysical Structure of Judgment and Aspiration*

Greetings, Sons of God. In today's advanced exploration, we delve into the profound metaphysical profile of the Apostle James, an embodiment of aspiration, mental elevation, and the divine faculty of judgment. As we dissect this archetype, we shall uncover how James signifies the mind's journey toward discernment and enlightenment, forming an integral part of each one of us as we pursue higher spiritual understanding. This profile is designed not merely as an academic exercise but as a transformative mirror—illuminating aspects of ourselves that must be honed and purified to align with the divine.

The Symbolism of James: The Air Element and the Mental Edifice

James represents the mental edifice of humanity, the structure of mind that rises through aspiration and enlightenment. Within the soul's journey, James is akin to the element of air—signifying the intellect, the capacity to rise above base instincts, and the instrument through which clarity and vision manifest. He is the "supplanter," one who displaces lower tendencies with higher aspirations. For the Sons of God, this archetype teaches us that our mental faculties are not fixed structures but dynamic entities meant to evolve and ascend.

James and the Faculty of Judgment

Central to James's archetype is the quality of judgment—a discerning, intellectual process that seeks balance and justice. This is not mere analytical thought but a higher order of perception rooted in spiritual illumination. Judgment, in this context, is tied to the solar plexus, the energy center that channels both power and perception. For us, the Sons of God, James represents the discerning power that evaluates our experiences with caution and introspection. However, he warns against the lower tendency to become ensnared in criticism, fear, and condemnation.

As spiritual aspirants, our task is to elevate this faculty, refining judgment through alignment with divine truth rather than worldly perspectives.

Aspiration and the Role of Spiritual Discrimination

James signifies a faculty that grows and matures through aspiration, an intrinsic pull toward higher realms of consciousness. This aspiration is not mere ambition; it is a yearning for spiritual illumination, a desire for the mind to be free from the shadows of materialism and ego. The journey of James as an apostle of Christ shows us the discipline of the mind, which must be trained to respond to the call of the Higher Self. As aspiring Sons of God, we are reminded that the quality of aspiration, when aligned with divine will, transforms personal ambition into spiritual excellence.

James as Judgment and Order

The dual symbolism of James—seen through James, son of Zebedee, and James, son of Alphaeus—reveals two facets of mental faculty: judgment and order. James, son of Zebedee, embodies the aspect of discernment, rooted in the solar plexus, while James, son of Alphaeus, represents order, seated in the navel. Together, they form a cohesive framework, reminding us that true judgment requires an internal order, a harmonious arrangement of thoughts and emotions. For the Sons of God, this duality encourages the cultivation of both discernment and organization within the mind, an alignment that leads to stability and clarity.

The Disciples as Spiritual Qualities and the Twelve-Fold Path

In the metaphysical perspective, the twelve apostles symbolize the twelve superior qualities or virtues within the soul, each an expression of divine faculties aligned with the Christ-consciousness. James, along with his fellow apostles, represents an aspect of this twelve-fold path, each quality existing in harmony to elevate the entire being. These twelve faculties act as a foundation, supporting the indwelling Christ, the divine spark within. For the Sons of God, recognizing these qualities as inherent spiritual tools is paramount in aligning with the Higher Self, transforming human tendencies into divine attributes.

Gethsemane: The Interior Garden of Self-Confrontation

The experience at Gethsemane, wherein Jesus took Peter, James, and John, symbolizes an inner state where the soul confronts its deepest challenges. In this metaphysical garden, James's faculty of reason stands alongside Peter's lower mind and John's love, symbolizing the convergence of thought, emotion, and willpower. Here, judgment is called to rise above the struggles of the lower self, to transcend the suffering born of egoic attachment. For us, the Sons of God, Gethsemane teaches the necessity of inner silence, a place where reason, love, and perseverance meet in quiet surrender to the divine.

The Transfiguration: Elevation and Inner Alchemy

The Transfiguration story holds profound symbolism in the journey of James. As a participant in this event, James is elevated to witness the harmonious integration of the ethical (Moses), the psychic (Elijah), and the divine (Christ) within himself. This represents an initiation, a mystical awakening where the lower faculties glimpse their highest potential in divine unity. For the Sons of God, the Transfiguration signifies the moment when intellectual discernment, rooted in James, begins to perceive the divine reality, understanding that true wisdom transcends mental boundaries.

Ambition and the Sublimation of Desire

The story of James and John's mother petitioning Jesus to place her sons at his right and left hand reveals a spiritual lesson in the sublimation of ambition. The desire to be exalted must be purified and transformed into a spiritual aspiration. True ambition, as shown by James, is not the attainment of worldly positions but an inner elevation, a striving to reach the divine.

For the Sons of God, this is a reminder that all worldly desires must be refined, aligning with the soul's higher purpose rather than personal gain.

Judgment in the Cosmic Structure: Disciples Seated upon Thrones

In the cosmic order, the apostles seated upon twelve thrones symbolize the elevation of disciplined qualities to their highest state, where they become judges over the lower faculties. Judgment, as embodied by James, reaches a divine maturity, where it governs not with criticism but with understanding and compassion. This state represents a perfected mind, elevated above the confines of mortal thinking, capable of discerning truth from illusion. For the Sons of God, this is the ultimate aim of judgment—to rise above duality, embodying divine justice in thought and action.

Conclusion: James as the Divine Faculty of Judgment and Aspiration

In conclusion, James is not merely a figure from religious texts but an archetype representing the divine faculty of judgment and aspiration within each of us. His journey reflects the mind's transformative process from mere intellectual analysis to a vessel of divine wisdom. For the Sons of God, James serves as an eternal reminder to elevate our thoughts, refine our judgments, and aspire beyond the limitations of the material plane. Through him, we are called to build the mental edifice of enlightenment, a temple where the Christ-consciousness can dwell in full glory.

In this journey, may we learn to balance our judgments with compassion, our aspirations with humility, and our mental faculties with divine purpose. James stands as a beacon, illuminating the path of disciplined intellect, guiding the Sons of God toward a harmonious union with the Higher Self. Let us carry this understanding into our inner work, knowing that, like James, we are each called to be architects of our own enlightenment.

Simon: *The Zealot as a Metaphysical Archetype*

In this lecture, we explore the metaphysical profile of Simon the Zealot, not as a historical figure, but as an archetype representing a deeply disciplined and fervent quality of the soul. Simon the Zealot embodies the zeal and ardent dedication necessary for the spiritual journey—a relentless, almost fiery commitment that symbolizes a transformative force within the Sons of God. To understand Simon metaphysically is to recognize within ourselves the capacity for unwavering passion in the pursuit of divine truth, an essential attribute on the path toward spiritual illumination.

Zeal as Purifying Fire

The quality of zeal attributed to Simon is not mere enthusiasm; it is an intense, disciplined drive that seeks alignment with the highest ideal—the Higher Self. This zeal can be likened to a purifying fire, one that seeks to burn away impurities, distractions, and attachments to lower desires. For the Sons of God, the metaphysical essence of Simon teaches the importance of channeling one's intense energies toward spiritual refinement and inner transformation. This is not about fanaticism or extremism in the material sense, but rather about developing a disciplined dedication to the inner work of the soul, a commitment to cultivating the attributes of divinity within.

Balancing Zeal with Compassion and Wisdom

Simon's zeal can be contrasted with the energies of other apostles to show the balance required on the spiritual path. While qualities like compassion (represented by John) or intellectual seeking (represented by Thomas) might appear in harmony with the gentle nurturing of the soul, Simon's zeal is the force that insists on unwavering focus and commitment. It is this intensity that pushes the soul forward in times of resistance, inspiring the Sons of God to confront and transcend inner and outer challenges.

The zeal of Simon calls upon the Higher Self to mobilize all faculties toward spiritual ascension, serving as a beacon that reminds the Sons of God that spiritual awakening requires an active, dynamic pursuit, not passive acceptance.

Integrating Zeal with Other Divine Qualities

In integrating Simon's zeal with other metaphysical qualities, such as the wisdom of Christ and the gentleness of John, we find a balanced pathway for the Sons of God. Zeal, when unchecked, can lead to impatience and potential dissonance within the soul. However, when combined with wisdom and compassion, it transforms into a focused, purposeful intensity, driving the soul with clarity and balance toward its ultimate realization. This balanced zeal enables the Sons of God to stand firm in the face of worldly temptations and distractions, empowering them to transcend the lower self and align with their divine purpose.

Spiritual Vigilance as an Expression of Zeal

Furthermore, Simon's zeal serves as a reminder of the need for spiritual vigilance. In the same way that Simon was known for his fervent dedication, the Sons of God are called to maintain a vigilant awareness of the inner workings of their mind and spirit. This vigilance is not fear-based but rooted in an understanding that the path to enlightenment is fraught with subtle traps and diversions. Simon's example teaches that only through constant attention and dedication can the soul avoid stagnation and continue to evolve.

Zeal as the Alchemical Fire of Transformation

The presence of zeal as a disciplined quality also speaks to the transformative potential within the Sons of God. By embracing Simon's archetype, the Sons of God learn to harness the force of their inner fire, directing it toward the higher planes of consciousness rather than letting it dissipate in the pursuits of the ego. Simon represents the alchemical fire of transformation—a process by which the lower nature is purified, refined, and transmuted into spiritual gold.

Conclusion: Zeal as a Guide on the Path of Divine Realization

In conclusion, the metaphysical profile of Simon the Zealot is one of disciplined passion, intense dedication, and transformative power. His zeal is the embodiment of the fiery commitment needed to traverse the path of enlightenment.

For the Sons of God, Simon's essence serves as a reminder that the spiritual journey demands a fervent dedication to truth and purity, urging them to embody this zeal within their own hearts as they walk the path of divine realization. In this way, Simon the Zealot stands as a guide, illuminating the path for those who seek to know and become their Highest Self.

John the Beloved: *The Alchemy of Divine Love and Spiritual Insight in the Path of the Sons of God*

Greetings, Sons of God. Today, we delve deeply into the metaphysical profile of John, an apostle whose qualities transcend his historical figure and invite us to embody divine love and wisdom within ourselves. Our exploration of John is not a mere historical reflection but an examination of the spiritual attributes that he symbolizes and how they resonate within us, the aspiring Sons of God.

Understanding John as an Archetype of Love and Spiritual Vision

In the metaphysical realm, John is not simply a disciple who loved Jesus; he represents the highest faculty of love within the soul—the love that transcends physical attachment and becomes a unifying force with the divine. John is often described as "the disciple whom Jesus loved," which points to his embodiment of divine love in its purest, unadulterated form. This is not the love that seeks or desires; it is love as a principle, an energy that aligns with truth and with the highest aspect of the self.

When the Sons of God examine the nature of this love, we must understand that it functions in two primary ways: as an active force that drives compassion and as an inner quality that fuels spiritual enlightenment. John represents the masculine, or positive, aspect of love, which takes action in the world.

Unlike passive love, which may observe and support, this active love seeks to transform, to reach out, and to bring light to the darker corners of the human experience.

John and the Spiritual Journey of Self-Purification

As the Sons of God, our journey is one of progressive self-purification, where we refine our intentions and actions to align with divine truth. John embodies the principle of purification through love—he shows us that love is the ultimate purifier of the soul. In moments of doubt or inner turmoil, it is love that dispels illusions and brings clarity to the mind.

To recognize John within ourselves is to acknowledge the part of our spiritual nature that seeks to cleanse and uplift. This purification process requires self-discipline, symbolized in John's devotion and unwavering loyalty. It is through this commitment to love and purity that the Sons of God can ascend to higher states of spiritual awareness, mirroring John's journey as one of the most enlightened of the apostles.

The Role of John in Dispelling the Lower Nature

John's metaphysical profile illustrates the journey of overcoming the lower mind's illusions and attachments. In many ways, he represents the soul's struggle to transcend the baser aspects of existence. By embracing love and inner wisdom, John teaches us to bring our lower nature into harmony with the higher self.

This is an essential lesson for the Sons of God, who seek not only knowledge but also the transformation of the lower self to be in alignment with divine ideals.

In John's metaphysical narrative, we observe the purification of desires and the redirection of the will. John calls us to transform the ego's desires into selfless service and divine love. He represents the ability to perceive truth beyond the veil of appearances, to see through the superficiality of the material world, and to witness the deeper spiritual truths that guide our existence.

John as the Embodiment of Spiritual Insight and Inner Peace

In addition to representing love, John symbolizes a profound level of spiritual insight—a divine perception that allows him to see the truth beyond material illusions. This insight is the foundation of inner peace, for it brings an understanding that all outer conflicts and tribulations are transitory. For the Sons of God, cultivating this insight means developing an unwavering trust in the spiritual process, a faith that guides us through the trials of existence.

John's peace comes from his alignment with divine will. He embodies the tranquility that emerges when one's life is in harmony with higher principles. This is a call to the Sons of God to seek inner harmony through alignment with divine will, to let go of resistance and to find serenity in the awareness that we are expressions of a higher purpose.

The Transmutation of the Lower Self through John's Example

The Sons of God are tasked with the transformation of the lower self—a journey that John exemplifies. John's unwavering faith and love allow him to transcend the constraints of the ego. This transcendence is essential for those on the path to spiritual mastery, for it allows us to overcome the limitations imposed by the lower nature.

To embody John is to cultivate the strength to face inner trials with love, to meet challenges without resentment, and to persist in the pursuit of spiritual truth regardless of external obstacles. John's life encourages the Sons of God to confront the shadows within themselves and to transmute them through the light of divine love.

Integrating John's Qualities into the Path of Enlightenment

As we progress in our journey as Sons of God, integrating John's qualities means embodying love as a transformative force. It is the love that inspires, uplifts, and awakens the divine within ourselves and others. It is the love that is unconditioned, unwavering, and aligned with truth.

John's example teaches us that this path requires courage—the courage to love unconditionally, to forgive freely, and to see beyond the illusions of separateness. This path is not for the faint-hearted; it is for those who dare to become vessels of divine love in a world that often resists it.

Conclusion: The Legacy of John for the Sons of God

In conclusion, the Apostle John stands as a beacon for the Sons of God, guiding us toward the ultimate realization of love and spiritual insight. John's metaphysical profile is a reminder that love is both the path and the destination. As we strive to embody his qualities, we find ourselves becoming conduits for divine love, illuminating the world with the light of higher truth.

Let the Sons of God take this understanding of John into their hearts, allowing his attributes to awaken within them. For it is through this awakening that we fulfill our purpose, becoming expressions of divine love, wisdom, and peace, just as John exemplified. Let this love guide us in our journey of enlightenment, empowering us to rise above the ego and embrace our true nature as Sons of God.

Andrew The Apostle: *Strength and the Astral Self*

Introduction: In our exploration of the metaphysical profiles of the apostles, we arrive at Andrew, whose qualities and symbolic significance provide profound insights for the spiritual journey of the 'Sons of God.' As we delve into Andrew's archetype, we consider him not just as a historical figure but as a metaphysical embodiment of strength, unity, and the astral self. Through understanding Andrew's attributes, we gain clarity on how his essence aligns with the Sons' path to enlightenment and inner transformation.

Andrew as the Embodiment of Strength and Unity

Andrew's name, rooted in the Greek for "a strong man," is more than a literal interpretation. In the metaphysical context, Andrew symbolizes the strength of mind—a manly, steadfast energy that finds joy in the inexhaustible Source of strength within. This inner power is not merely physical but spiritual, representing an enduring vitality that allows one to proclaim, "We have found the Messiah."

This strength is intrinsically connected to faith, as exemplified by Andrew's relationship with his brother, Simon Peter. While Peter represents the capacity for faith, Andrew embodies the strength that upholds and manifests that faith. In the metaphysical journey, strength and faith are intertwined, creating a bond of unity in the mind. This unity is a powerful tool for the Sons of God, as it establishes a resilience that transcends adverse experiences, grounding the spiritual seeker in the strength derived from the divine source.

The Astral Self and Andrew's Symbolism

Andrew's symbolic resonance extends into the astral realm, often associated with the astral body or subjective self. The astral self represents the bridge between the physical and higher spiritual states, managing sensory experiences and ordinary practical functions. In the context of Andrew, the astral self is depicted as an agent of adaptation, responsible for aligning the senses and emotions to the requirements of daily life.

For the Sons of God, the astral self, embodied by Andrew, becomes a directive force that must be disciplined and aligned with the higher spiritual principles. This aspect of Andrew suggests the need to control the sympathetic nervous system, grounding the self in calm strength. Andrew's association with "water" further reinforces his role as a conduit between the higher and lower planes, symbolizing the fluid adaptability necessary to navigate the astral plane's mutable nature.

The Influence of Moral and Spiritual Figures on the Astral Self

The astral self, represented by Andrew, is influenced by both moral (John) and spiritual (Jesus) forces. In the metaphysical framework, these influences symbolize the dual guidance required to ascend from lower instincts toward divine consciousness.

Andrew's presence alongside John the Baptist and Jesus suggests that the Sons of God must integrate both the moral purification symbolized by John and the spiritual elevation represented by Jesus.

For the Sons, the astral self (Andrew) serves as an ally to the lower mind (Peter), balancing the moral and spiritual dimensions within the individual. This integration allows for the creation of a harmonious self that is both resilient in faith and fortified in strength, essential for traversing the spiritual journey toward enlightenment.

The Role of the Lower Mind and the Challenge of Separateness

In the journey of the Sons of God, the lower mind, symbolized by Peter, often stands as a barrier to the higher aspirations prompted by the Higher Self. Andrew's relationship with Peter highlights the struggle between the divine promptings of the Higher Ego and the resistance of the lower mind, which clings to doubt and error.

The story of Peter rebuking Jesus, where he fails to comprehend the "things of God," illustrates this internal conflict. Andrew, embodying the strength of mind, represents the capacity to confront and transcend the limitations imposed by the lower mind's sense of separateness. This is a crucial lesson for the Sons of God, as it underscores the importance of cultivating inner strength to overcome doubt, unify the self, and embrace the soul's higher aspirations.

The Astral Plane and the Symbolism of Water

In metaphysical symbolism, water often represents the astral plane—the domain of illusions, reflections, and the inverted truths of higher realities. Andrew's association with water emphasizes his role as a figure who navigates the astral plane's currents. This plane is rife with the "errors and illusions" that obscure the truth, challenging the spiritual seeker to distinguish between the transient reflections of truth and the eternal essence within.

For the Sons of God, understanding Andrew's role as a navigator of the astral waters is essential. It highlights the importance of transcending the astral plane's deceptions, using strength of mind to pierce through illusions and uncover the truths that reside in the deeper, spiritual planes.

The Vestures of the Soul and Their Role in Spiritual Ascent

The astral self functions within a framework of "vestures" or bodies, each corresponding to different levels of consciousness. Andrew's role as a guide through the astral plane aligns with these vestures, which serve as vehicles for the soul's evolution. The five vestures—Beatific, Cognitional, Sensorial, Vital, and Nutrimentitious—represent stages in the soul's journey from physicality to the sublime consciousness of the Divine.

The Sons of God must recognize Andrew's influence within the Sensorial vesture, as this is the plane where impressions from the senses are received and processed.

The strength Andrew embodies enables the Sons to maintain clarity and composure within the lower planes, while gradually ascending through the higher vestures of consciousness, ultimately reaching the Beatific vesture associated with divine union.

Transmutation of Desire and the Agricultural Caste (Vaisya)

In the symbolic language of spiritual growth, the Vaisya or agricultural caste represents the transformation of desire into a more refined, cultivated form. Andrew's association with this caste reflects the process of nurturing and disciplining the desire-nature within the astral body. This is not merely suppression but a deliberate transmutation, where lower emotions are sublimated into spiritual aspiration.

For the Sons of God, this teaching emphasizes the necessity of transmuting base desires into higher intentions aligned with the spiritual law. This practice of cultivating the inner "land" mirrors the agricultural metaphor, where the astral self is disciplined to yield the "fruits" of divine wisdom and strength.

Conclusion: Andrew as the Path of Strength and Unity for the Sons of God

In Andrew, the Sons of God find a model of inner strength, unity, and transcendence of the astral plane. His metaphysical profile reveals the necessity of integrating strength with faith, controlling the astral self, and overcoming the illusions of the lower mind.

By embracing Andrew's qualities, the Sons can navigate the path of spiritual enlightenment with resilience, ultimately embodying the strength required to reach divine unity.

This advanced metaphysical understanding of Andrew serves as a beacon for the Sons of God, guiding them to recognize and embody these divine attributes within themselves. As they journey through the vestures of the soul and the challenges of the astral plane, Andrew's strength will remain a testament to the enduring power of the Higher Self.

Peter: *Unveiling the Rock - The Metaphysical Archetype and The Pillar of Inner Divinity*

Greetings, Sons of God. This lecture is an in-depth exploration of the metaphysical profile of the Apostle Peter, designed to illuminate the divine archetype he represents within each of us. Our purpose here is to reveal not only the characteristics of Peter but also how these attributes act as an archetype within each of us, guiding us on the path of spiritual growth and enlightenment. This profile should be viewed as a transformative mirror, reflecting the inner work necessary to achieve the qualities of divine wisdom, resilience, and harmony with higher consciousness. This is not a mere historical recounting; it's an illumination of metaphysical truths embedded in ancient texts and symbols, framed to elevate one's understanding of self.

The Symbolism of Peter: The Lower Mind and the Journey to Transcendence

Peter, often portrayed as the representative of the lower mind, embodies the faculties that begin with limited understanding yet hold the potential for divine realization. In metaphysical terms, Peter signifies the initial, unrefined mental state that must undergo transformation to align with higher truths. This lower mind, symbolized by Peter, is not devoid of value; rather, it possesses the faculties of inquiry, resilience, and adaptability, albeit at a more nascent stage.

It seeks knowledge laboriously, often confined by earthly definitions and separations, as seen in the "tabernacles" or "compartments" that Peter desires to construct to house spiritual ideas separately.

This compartmentalizing tendency represents our inclination to isolate aspects of consciousness, dividing them into manageable segments rather than integrating them into a holistic understanding. For the Sons of God, this reflects an initial stage of spiritual journeying, where thoughts are categorized into moral (Moses), emotional (Elijah), and spiritual (Christ) sections, each in its own tabernacle.

Recognizing this tendency within ourselves allows us to understand the journey of uniting these compartments into a single, undivided awareness.

The Transfiguration and Inner Alchemy

Peter's role in the story of the Transfiguration illustrates the transformative process of raising the lower nature in alignment with the higher self. This event symbolizes an initiation—a profound awakening in which the lower mind (Peter) witnesses the harmonious integration of the ethical, emotional, and spiritual natures, personified by Moses, Elijah, and Christ. Here, Peter is exposed to the potential of transcendence, a vision of what it means for the soul to embody higher vibrations and radiate inner light. For the Sons of God, this signifies the moment when the lower, individualized self begins to dissolve its rigid boundaries, perceiving the divine unity within.

The appearance of Moses and Elijah alongside Christ in this event speaks to the confluence of body, mind, and heart, where each must be purified and uplifted. The Sons of God are called to recognize this trinity within themselves and engage in the inner alchemy required to transmute their earthly nature into divine consciousness. This requires an awareness that the "white raiment" symbolizes purity—a purification process that must occur in the mind, emotions, and spirit.

Faith as the Rock: Peter's Inner Strength

The newly added images emphasize the spiritual significance of Peter's unwavering faith, likened to a "rock." Faith is not simply a passive belief but a foundational principle that holds firm in adversity. Peter's transformation from Simon (meaning "hearing" or "receptivity") to Peter ("rock" or "stone") highlights this inner solidity. In metaphysical terms, Peter as "rock" represents the ability of the mind to stabilize and ground itself in spiritual truths.

This faith is the bedrock upon which spiritual consciousness builds, a steady foundation amidst the fluctuations of the earthly mind.

The Sons of God are reminded that Peter's faith, while initially wavering, becomes the grounding force that enables spiritual growth. This inner rock must be forged through experiences of doubt, denial, and reconnection, reflecting the journey from instability to divine certainty.

As we cultivate this steadfastness, the lower mind is no longer tossed by the "boisterous waves" of worldly thought, but instead, it anchors itself in higher wisdom.

Tribute Money: Balancing Earthly and Spiritual Obligations

In the allegory of the tribute money, Peter is once again emblematic of the lower mind grappling with the demands of material life versus spiritual commitments. The story explores the delicate balance of earthly obligations and spiritual pursuits. Christ's guidance here implies that while we exist in a material world, we are not bound by it. For the Sons of God, this is a call to harmonize practical responsibilities with the overarching quest for spiritual ascension, acknowledging that worldly duties should serve as stepping stones rather than chains.

In this light, the lower mind (Peter) is not to be dismissed or overcome by force but is to be trained and aligned with higher purposes. The experiences, facts (fish), and knowledge gathered from the world are essential for spiritual maturation. This symbolizes the need to approach earthly life not with attachment but with a sense of purpose aligned with divine will, understanding that the mundane can serve as a foundation for spiritual elevation.

Horses with Long Flowing Manes: The Lower Mind in Pursuit of Truth

The imagery of "horses with long flowing manes" further elucidates the faculties of the lower mind. Horses, with their strength and endurance, symbolize the lower mind's persistent, albeit laborious, search for truth. This is a journey of patience and gentleness, a grace that is learned over time as one wrestles with the limits of logical inquiry. For the Sons of God, this represents the discipline needed to temper the lower mind, transforming its unrelenting curiosity into an instrument of divine wisdom.

In the Sons' spiritual journey, the lower mind's persistence can either be a hindrance or a guiding force, depending on how it is channeled. It is through this refinement process that the lower faculties are elevated, embodying a gentler and more receptive quality, essential for the gradual revelation of higher truths.

The Net for the Catching of Fish: The Mechanism of Sensation and Aspiration

The concept of the "net for catching fish" is a metaphor for the astral mechanism behind sensory perception. This net collects sensations, which are then processed by the ego into differentiated experiences. Here, Peter, as the fisherman, represents the mind's task of sifting through worldly impressions, discerning spiritual truth from illusion. The act of casting the net signifies the gathering of knowledge and experiences, which serve as the building blocks of spiritual growth. The Sons of God are encouraged to recognize that their senses are tools, not ends in themselves, serving the soul's aspiration toward higher consciousness.

Satan as Limitation and Ignorance

In his struggle with limitation, Peter also encounters the concept of "Satan," symbolizing darkness, ignorance, and the boundaries of relativity (Saturn). Satan here is not a being of inherent evil but represents the barriers within the mind that must be transcended. For the Sons of God, this aspect of Peter's journey is a reminder that ignorance is the true adversary, and enlightenment—the casting away of darkness—is achieved through disciplined pursuit of knowledge and self-realization. Satan, then, is the projection of our inner limitations, and the act of overcoming it is an intrinsic part of the Christ-like journey within.

The Messiah and the Higher Self Within

Peter's realization of the "Messiah" is symbolic of recognizing the incoming Truth and Love that represents the Higher Self. The Messiah is the spark of divine insight that awakens within the soul, guiding it beyond the confines of the lower mind. This is a moment of spiritual recognition, where Peter, as an embodiment of each individual's journey, moves from mere follower to a conscious participant in divine will. For the Sons of God, the Messiah signifies the indwelling Christ-consciousness, the Higher Self that must be realized and allowed to govern one's being.

This recognition demands an internal "fiery purgation," a transformative burning away of the ego's impurities, leaving behind only that which is aligned with divine truth. In acknowledging this Higher Self, the Sons of God are called to embody the Messiah within themselves, realizing their inherent connection to the divine source.

In conclusion, the Apostle Peter serves as an archetype for the transformative journey of the lower mind toward enlightenment. Through him, we see the qualities of resilience, curiosity, and the potential for spiritual elevation. Each stage of Peter's journey—from compartmentalization to the Transfiguration, from balancing earthly duties to recognizing the Messiah within—offers profound insights for the Sons of God.

Peter's path is the path of every soul seeking union with the divine. It is a journey that begins with limitation and ignorance, symbolized by the lower mind, and progresses through disciplined striving and inner purification. Ultimately, it culminates in the realization of the Higher Self, the Christ-consciousness that resides within all. The Sons of God are encouraged to see Peter not just as a historical figure but as a metaphysical blueprint for their own spiritual transformation, embodying divine qualities and recognizing the potential to ascend beyond the confines of the lower nature into the light of higher awareness.

Thaddeus: *The Heart of Divine Release and the Pathway to Inner Illumination*

In this lecture, we will explore the profound metaphysical meaning behind the Apostle Thaddeus, also known as Jude or Judas, son of James, and how his qualities serve as a mirror to the divine attributes that the Sons of God are called to recognize and embody within themselves. As we delve into Thaddeus's role in spiritual elimination, we uncover the essential process of inner purification that each Son of God must undertake on the path to enlightenment. Thaddeus represents not just a figure of courage and compassion, but an embodiment of the transformative power of release—letting go of the outdated patterns and energies that obstruct one's true nature. Through understanding Thaddeus's qualities and his unique role, the Sons of God will see how these attributes apply directly to their journey, enabling them to refine their spiritual essence, clear away limitations, and prepare themselves to embody the light and love of the Christ consciousness.

Thaddeus as the Faculty of Elimination

Thaddeus, whose name denotes courage, warmth, and heart-centeredness, represents the metaphysical principle of elimination. In this context, elimination is not merely a physical process but a profound mental and spiritual cleansing. For the Sons of God, understanding Thaddeus as an emblem of the eliminative faculty means recognizing the importance of releasing thoughts, beliefs, and energies that no longer serve their divine path.

The eliminative faculty, located in the lower back, is instrumental in removing the accumulated mental and emotional residues that hinder spiritual growth. This process is essential for aspiring Sons of God, as it facilitates the space necessary for divine inspiration to enter.

The Power of Letting Go

In the metaphysical journey, letting go is a vital step toward enlightenment. Thaddeus embodies the capacity to relinquish outdated patterns and attachments that inhibit the Sons of God from actualizing their highest potential. This faculty is not simply a passive release; it is an active surrender of limiting beliefs, ego-driven desires, and fears.

The Sons of God must learn that true spiritual power lies in the ability to embrace new ideas, energies, and ways of being without clinging to past limitations. By doing so, they allow divine wisdom to flow through them unimpeded, purifying their consciousness and making space for spiritual truths.

Thaddeus and the Heart-Centered Courage

Thaddeus's qualities—large-heartedness, courage, and warmth—reflect a deeply compassionate nature. In metaphysical terms, courage does not merely denote fearlessness in the face of danger; it signifies the spiritual strength to face oneself, to confront inner shadows, and to transcend egoic fears. For the Sons of God, Thaddeus's courage is an invitation to cultivate a warm-hearted approach to spiritual practice, to cultivate self-compassion, and to hold space for transformation without judgment.

This courage, rooted in the heart, is foundational for those who seek to embody divine love. It is the courage to let go of lower inclinations and ascend toward the divine virtues that align with the Christ consciousness.

Balancing Receiving and Giving

Thaddeus symbolizes a harmonious balance between receiving and giving, holding and releasing. This balance is essential for the Sons of God, as it teaches the importance of reciprocity in spiritual practices. As they receive divine wisdom and insights, they must also give—both to others and to their own evolving selves.

In practical terms, this dynamic of holding and releasing is reflected in a balanced life. The Sons of God are called to cultivate inner peace through the conscious management of mental, emotional, and spiritual resources. Thaddeus's presence as a guiding archetype encourages them to embrace this flow, to be neither overly attached nor excessively detached, but to remain grounded in love and clarity.

The Inner Elimination of Fear, Hate, and Revenge

Thaddeus teaches that for the Sons of God to embody higher virtues, they must first cleanse themselves of lower emotional residues—fear, hate, revenge, and other limiting energies. These emotions disrupt the harmony within the mind and body, blocking the flow of spiritual energy.

Through metaphysical elimination, these lower vibrations are transmuted. Love, tenderness, and an unwavering courage become the dominant forces, aligning the Sons of God with their divine purpose. Thaddeus's role here is transformative; he encourages an inward purification, inviting his followers to discard emotional burdens that hinder their ascent.

Thaddeus as the Archetype of Transcendence

For the Sons of God, Thaddeus is more than an apostle; he is a spiritual archetype representing the power to transcend earthly limitations. This transcendence is achieved not by escaping the material world, but by refining one's relationship with it. As Thaddeus discards the non-essential, he rises closer to the essential truth of divine nature.

In this way, Thaddeus embodies the transcendental potential that each Son of God holds within. The process of eliminating what is unnecessary is not just a removal; it is an ascension, a rising into the higher realms of thought and consciousness.

Integrating Other Divine Aspects through Elimination

As the Sons of God deepen their journey, Thaddeus's metaphysical elimination opens the path to integrating qualities from other divine figures and apostles. By purifying their vessel, they make room to embody attributes from other enlightened beings, harmonizing with divine aspects of faith, wisdom, love, and courage.

Thaddeus's elimination process becomes a foundation for integration. As the Sons of God shed the lower attributes, they can seamlessly incorporate the higher virtues, embodying the holistic and unified qualities of divinity. Each act of elimination is a step toward divine wholeness, preparing them to mirror the light of the Christ within.

Thaddeus as the Gateway to Christ Consciousness

In the metaphysical hierarchy of transformation, Thaddeus stands as a crucial gatekeeper. His faculty of elimination is not an end but a beginning—a preparatory purification that leads the Sons of God to the threshold of Christ consciousness. Without Thaddeus's eliminative power, they would be weighed down by the impurities of the lower self.

As they embody Thaddeus's principles, the Sons of God prepare to ascend into their highest nature. Thaddeus is thus not only a model of courage and warmth but a vital bridge, a force that clears the path for divine realization. Through him, they come to understand that elimination is not merely the discarding of the old but an essential act of rebirth—a continuous cycle of death and resurrection within, culminating in the full realization of the Christ consciousness.

Side Note: *The Metaphysical Significance of Thaddeus' Alternate Name, Jude, and His Connection to James*

In exploring the metaphysical dimensions of Thaddeus, who is also known as Jude, we uncover a profound symbolic meaning tied to his role as the apostle representing elimination. The alternate name, "Jude," which shares its origin with "Judah" and "Judas," denotes "praise Jehovah" or a recognition of divine essence. This name shift carries a unique metaphysical insight, emphasizing the dual aspect of his role in both releasing and honoring divine energies. By using "Jude," this aspect highlights the process of acknowledgment and release, suggesting that true spiritual elimination is not merely about letting go but is also an act of reverent recognition, a purposeful surrender to the divine will.

In metaphysical terms, the name "Jude" symbolizes a refined faculty of consciousness that actively praises or aligns with higher truth. This is not an ordinary release but a release that honors divine order, making space for higher qualities to manifest within. Through Jude's name, we see elimination elevated to an act of reverence, where surrender becomes transformative, allowing divine light to permeate the consciousness.

The Brotherly Connection of Jude and James

Jude is identified as the brother of James, which adds another layer of metaphysical insight. James, representing the faculty of judgment or discernment, is closely linked with Jude, the faculty of elimination. This connection signifies the interdependence between judgment and elimination. For one to exercise true discernment (James), there must be an ability to release or eliminate that which no longer serves the soul's highest purpose (Jude). This sibling relationship indicates that the faculty of discernment is incomplete without the complementary action of letting go.

In this sense, the relationship between Jude and James is an allegory for the inner workings of spiritual growth. Judgment alone, without the power to release, can lead to stagnation or attachment to outdated patterns. Conversely, elimination without discernment may lead to indiscriminate rejection. Together, these faculties work harmoniously to guide the soul on its journey, discerning what is needed and eliminating what is not, ensuring a balanced approach to spiritual evolution. Thus, Jude and James reflect the twin forces of letting go and wise discernment, both essential for the aspirant on the path of self-realization.

6th Entry

ChristHood (Jesus) and the Sun of God:
Part One

The journey of Christ Hood, as revealed through Jesus, is a profound ascent into divine consciousness—a transformation from the limitations of the lower self to the realization of one's true identity as a Son of God. This process, rooted deeply in the metaphysical principles of unity, transcendence, and divine self-realization, serves as a spiritual template for humanity's potential to embody the Christ-nature within. In becoming the Son of God, Jesus does not merely represent an isolated figure of sanctity but rather the archetypal blueprint for every soul's journey toward its highest purpose. This journey is marked by an alignment with divine law, a liberation from the desires of the lower nature, and a conscious merging with the essence of the Higher Self.

The Divine Structure of the Soul

The divine structure of the soul as presented in the teachings aligns with the multi-dimensional layers of human existence—spiritual, mental, astral, and physical. In Jesus, these dimensions are unified and perfected, symbolizing the transcendence of separation and the embodiment of divine purpose. The "divine structure" emphasizes the dual aspects of man: the Higher Self (or Divine Spark) and the incarnate human form. Jesus, as the Son of God, exists as the bridge between these planes, harmonizing the eternal Spirit with the temporal form.

This structure enables the Son of God to act as both a channel for divine wisdom and as an example of perfected human nature.

- *Spiritual Plane (Buddhic and Causal)*: At the highest level, the Son of God embodies the Buddhic consciousness, or the "Divine Ray." This consciousness is both an individual expression and an extension of the Absolute, manifesting pure awareness, compassion, and unity.
- *Mental and Astral Planes*: In the middle planes, the Son of God exemplifies mastery over the mind and emotions. Jesus embodies the alignment of the mental body with divine intelligence, signifying the soul's potential to purify and transcend personal ego in service to the Higher Self.
- *Physical Plane*: Jesus' earthly form is not merely a physical vessel but a sanctified "temple" through which divine works are manifested. His actions and teachings are expressions of the soul's divine intelligence operating within the human frame, demonstrating the potential for physical embodiment to act as a sacred instrument of spiritual truth.

The Symbolism of the Birth of Christ

The birth of Jesus, symbolized through narratives of humility and sanctification, represents the inception of Christ-consciousness within the soul. This "birth" is not merely an event in historical terms but a timeless archetype for the spiritual awakening that can occur within every individual. The virginity of Mary signifies the purity of the soul, untainted by lower desires, prepared to receive the divine essence. Wrapped in swaddling clothes and laid in a manger, the Christ-child symbolizes the humble and unassuming nature of divine wisdom in its early stages, contained within the simplicity of human experience before it expands into its fullness.

Macarius and Methodius highlight the inner union of the Logos with "pious souls," suggesting that the Christ is born within each individual who aligns with the divine. Thus, Jesus' birth becomes an allegory for the inner birth of divinity within us—a state of consciousness that grows and matures as we, too, nurture our divine potential.

The Journey of Transcendence: "Christ Must Increase, But John Must Decrease"

The statement, "Christ must increase, but John must decrease," encapsulates the path of spiritual evolution as one moves from a moral or law-bound consciousness to a state of divine love and truth. John represents the moral aspects of the soul, the preparatory phase wherein the soul is disciplined and aligned with the principles of righteousness. However, as the Christ-consciousness rises within, it transcends and subsumes the moralistic framework, entering a state where love, wisdom, and spiritual insight become the guiding forces.

The Son of God, as symbolized in Jesus, reveals the progressive dissolution of the lower nature, making way for the influx of divine wisdom and love. This transition signifies the ascension of spiritual attributes over the moral and ethical, evolving the soul's orientation from outward conformity to an inward realization of divine identity.

The Two Birds and the Tree of Life: Higher and Lower Selves

In ancient teachings, the imagery of two birds perched on the "Tree of Life" represents the Higher Self (Paramatman) and the Incarnate Self (Jivatman). One bird, enjoying the fruits of worldly experience, symbolizes the incarnate human soul, which engages with the material realm, while the other bird, a silent watcher, represents the divine witness, the eternal aspect within each being that remains untouched by temporal experiences.

In the life of Jesus, this relationship between the Higher and Lower Selves is perfected; he exemplifies the integration of the silent, observing Self with the active, compassionate self engaged in the world. The Higher Self, seated above, observes the earthly self as it moves through cycles of experience and learning, ultimately guiding it toward spiritual unity. Jesus' life, teachings, and sacrifices symbolize the path for every soul to transcend duality, achieving harmony between the indwelling Self and the transcendent Divine.

The Christ Principle: The Integration of Atma-Buddhi

Christ-consciousness is understood as the manifestation of the Atma-Buddhi—the divine intelligence and spirit animating human consciousness. Jesus embodies this principle through the divine mission, expressing love, wisdom, and truth not as separate acts but as the seamless outflow of a unified, divine consciousness. The Christ Principle is the spiritual force that propels the soul toward enlightenment, lifting it above the realm of personal desire and material limitations.

This principle is illustrated in the statement, "As a branch cannot bear fruit of itself except it abide in the vine, no more can ye except ye abide in me." Here, Jesus speaks to the necessity of alignment with the Christ-consciousness for spiritual vitality, suggesting that divine wisdom, peace, and joy arise naturally when one's lower self is surrendered to the Higher Self.

Christ's Second Coming: Inner Realization Over Literal Expectation

The "second coming" is often misinterpreted as an external event; however, from a metaphysical perspective, it represents the final stage of soul purification and ascent, where the individual consciousness fully merges with the divine. This culmination marks the soul's ascension from material bondage to spiritual liberty, symbolized by Christ's return "in glory." The lifting of heads, as referenced in the text, speaks to the upward aspiration of the soul, as it is liberated from lower consciousness.

Jesus' teachings emphasize the need for internal resurrection —a rising of the Christ within each soul, which brings about spiritual maturity and the fulfillment of divine potential. This process is a gradual, inner transformation, where the soul progressively reflects the qualities of the divine, embodying wisdom, love, and unity as part of its essential nature.

Conclusion: The Path of the Sun of God

Through these stages, Jesus serves as the exemplar of the Son of God—a state of being that transcends ordinary human limitations and embodies the divine. This journey toward Christ Hood is open to every soul willing to transcend the lower nature and align fully with the Higher Self. The Son of God, then, is not a distant ideal but a present reality, waiting to be awakened within. As we study and reflect upon the path of Jesus, we are reminded that each step taken in truth, compassion, and unity is a step toward realizing the divine potential within ourselves, fulfilling the true purpose of human existence.

ChristHood and the Sun of God: *Part Two*

The Divine Manifestation of Christ Consciousness in the Son of God

In the second half of our exploration of Christ Hood, we delve into the profound dimensions of divine sonship, understanding Christ as both a cosmic and internal phenomenon. The Christ Principle embodied by Jesus transcends historical or religious boundaries, acting as a metaphysical guide for the "Sons of God"—those who recognize and strive toward their divine potential. Here, we will dissect the layers of the divine consciousness that Christ represents, focusing on the metaphysical implications of Jesus as the Son of God and how this archetype applies to the journey of the soul toward enlightenment. By examining the Christ Consciousness in its entirety, we aim to illuminate the path for each soul to realize its true nature as a beacon of divine light.

The Image of God and Divine Projections

The phrase "Image of God" signifies more than a mere likeness; it is a projection of divine attributes within the highest planes of the soul, manifesting as Love, Wisdom, and Truth. This image is not confined to physical characteristics but refers to the soul's alignment with divine qualities. The Son of God embodies this image, becoming a vessel for divine Love (Atma) and Wisdom (Buddhi) united in mind (Manas). As the archetype of divine man, Jesus demonstrates the fusion of divine and human realms, offering humanity a template for achieving union with the Godhead.

The Image of God within each individual represents the dual nature of existence: the human aspect, bound to earthly experiences, and the divine aspect, seeking unity with the Infinite. This duality is resolved in the Christ, who operates in perfect harmony with divine law. The Sons of God are thus encouraged to recognize this divine image within themselves, transcending limitations to embody divine Love and Wisdom as foundational truths.

The Essence of Godhead: Absolute Reality and Infinite Potential

The Godhead is the unmanifested source, the Absolute Reality that encompasses all potentialities. It is the boundless, eternal origin from which all forms and expressions of life arise. Within this absolute realm, beyond human comprehension, exists the divine source that both transcends and permeates creation. Jesus, as the Son of God, emerges from this Infinite Source, representing the manifested aspect of the unmanifested Godhead.

The Godhead, being beyond duality, is the unity that subsumes all opposites, and Christ embodies this unity, bringing it forth into the material world. The Sons of God, in aspiring to this divine union, are called to perceive beyond the transient forms of existence and attune to the Godhead within. In so doing, they approach the infinite mystery that underlies all creation, recognizing their essence as rooted in this divine reality.

The Path of Incarnation and the Divine Descent

Incarnation is a descent into matter, an act of divine will to bring forth higher consciousness into the lower planes of existence. The Son of God, represented by Jesus, chooses to incarnate not out of necessity but out of love for humanity and a desire to guide souls back to the divine. This descent is marked by the voluntary acceptance of human limitations while maintaining a connection to the divine essence.

In the journey of Christ Hood, incarnation becomes a sacred path where divine attributes are revealed through human actions. Jesus' life illustrates how divinity can operate within human constraints, transforming them into vehicles for spiritual evolution. The Sons of God are therefore reminded that their own incarnations are opportunities to reflect divine qualities, transforming earthly experiences into expressions of divine love and wisdom.

Divine Wisdom and the Logos: The Creative Word

The Logos, or Divine Word, represents the creative power that emanates from the Godhead to bring forth all things. Jesus, as the incarnation of the Logos, reveals the power of divine speech, where spoken truth resonates with the essence of creation. The Logos is not merely a word but the living expression of divine intention, embodying wisdom, love, and purpose in perfect harmony.

The Sons of God are called to align their words and actions with the Logos, understanding that true speech is an act of creation. By cultivating purity in thought, word, and deed, they participate in the ongoing creative process of the universe. In doing so, they align with the cosmic order, allowing divine wisdom to manifest through their lives as a reflection of the Logos.

The Holy Spirit and Divine Breath: Feminine Aspect of the Divine

The Holy Spirit, or Divine Breath, symbolizes the feminine aspect of the Divine Trinity, representing the nurturing and life-giving force that animates creation. It proceeds from the Godhead as a sacred energy that sustains all beings. Jesus, in union with the Holy Spirit, demonstrates the balanced integration of masculine and feminine aspects within the divine nature. This union is essential for the full expression of Christ Consciousness, where compassion and strength, wisdom and understanding, operate as one.

For the Sons of God, the Holy Spirit acts as a guide, inspiring them to cultivate the divine feminine within—qualities of compassion, intuition, and nurturing love. This integration allows for a complete embodiment of Christ Consciousness, balancing action with receptivity, will with wisdom. By opening to the Holy Spirit, they attune to the subtle, nurturing aspect of divine presence, allowing it to flow through their lives as a healing and transformative force.

The Baptism of Fire: Purification and Spiritual Illumination

The baptism of fire is a symbol of purification, where the lower self is consumed, and the divine essence emerges in its true form. This fire is not a destructive force but an illuminative one, representing the divine energy that purifies the soul. Jesus' baptism with the Holy Spirit and fire signifies this transformative process, where the ego is dissolved, and the divine nature is revealed.

The Sons of God, in undergoing their own baptism of fire, are called to embrace this purification as an essential step in spiritual awakening. Through the trials and challenges that life presents, they burn away attachments, fears, and illusions, emerging as vessels of divine light. This process is a testament to the power of divine love, which refines and elevates the soul to its highest potential, allowing it to shine forth with clarity and truth.

Divine Union and the Tree of Life: Transcending Duality

The Tree of Life symbolizes the interconnectedness of all existence, where the roots and branches represent the ascent and descent of divine consciousness. Jesus, as the Son of God, embodies the ultimate union of the Higher and Lower Selves, transcending duality and achieving perfect alignment with divine will. This union is the culmination of the Christ journey, where individual identity merges with the universal, and the soul is restored to its divine origin.

For the Sons of God, the Tree of Life serves as a reminder of their own path toward unity with the Divine. By aligning their lives with the principles of truth, love, and wisdom, they cultivate the inner balance necessary to transcend duality. In this state of divine union, they become living embodiments of the Christ, reflecting the interconnectedness of all beings and the infinite love that sustains creation.

The Final Realization: Christ Consciousness as the Fulfillment of Divine Potential

The journey of Christ Hood culminates in the full realization of Christ Consciousness, where the individual self is wholly absorbed into the divine. This is the "second coming" of Christ within the soul, not as an external event but as an internal awakening. Jesus, in his resurrection, demonstrates this final stage, where death and limitations of the physical realm are transcended, revealing the eternal nature of the divine Self. For the Sons of God, this realization represents the ultimate fulfillment of their spiritual journey, where all aspects of their being are unified with the divine purpose.

In embodying Christ Consciousness, they become conduits of divine love, wisdom, and power, living testimonies to the transformative potential within every soul. This state of being is not merely an ideal but a present reality, accessible to all who are willing to surrender the ego and embrace their true identity as Sons of God.

Conclusion: Christ Hood as the Path of Enlightenment

The Christ Principle, as exemplified by Jesus, reveals the path of enlightenment available to every soul. By embodying the divine attributes of love, wisdom, and unity, the Sons of God walk in the footsteps of Christ, not as mere followers but as active participants in the divine mystery. Through their journey of self-discovery, purification, and divine union, they reveal the infinite potential within, shining as beacons of light for others on the path.

As we conclude this lecture, let it serve as a reminder that Christ Hood is not an exclusive state but an invitation for all. It is the birthright of every soul to awaken to its divine nature, transcending limitations and embodying the light of the divine. The journey of Christ Hood is both a return to the source and an evolution of the soul—a testament to the enduring love of the Godhead that calls each soul to rise, transform, and fulfill its highest purpose. In this, the Sons of God recognize their role in the cosmic dance, living as reflections of the Divine, united in the eternal Christ Consciousness.

7th Entry

The Sun of God in the Metaphysical Framework (Enhanced with Hindu Perspectives)

To truly understand the concept of the "Son of God" in its fullest metaphysical depth, we must look beyond conventional definitions and explore the layers of spiritual symbolism embedded within this archetype. The "Son of God" is not merely a historical figure or a religious title; it is a profound principle woven into the fabric of the universe and inherent within each soul. This archetype finds resonance across spiritual traditions, including the Hindu pantheon, where deities like **Vishnu**—the preserver of cosmic order—embody the sustaining divine energy, while avatars like **Krishna** and **Rama** represent the descent of the divine into human form, guiding humanity toward enlightenment. As we dive into this exploration, we will examine the symbolic connections to divine energies, universal laws, and spiritual growth, incorporating these deities as embodiments of the eternal truths expressed in the "Son of God."

The Incarnation of Souls and the Descent into Humanity

The "Son of God" represents the divine descent, the embodiment of the Supreme Self within the confines of human form. At the heart of this concept lies the idea of the Divine Monad, the original essence from which all souls emerge. Each soul is a fragment of this original divine source, descending into human existence to experience, evolve, and ultimately return to its spiritual origin. This descent mirrors the role of **Krishna** and **Rama**, avatars of Vishnu, who incarnate in the material world to restore balance and guide humanity towards dharma (cosmic order). Krishna's life, filled with wisdom and playfulness (lila), symbolizes the divine's engagement with creation, teaching that the descent into material form is a sacred journey rather than a fall.

As the soul incarnates, it becomes obscured by the limitations of earthly desires and sensory experiences. However, through conscious evolution, these latent divine qualities are gradually awakened. The journey of each soul mirrors that of the "Son of God," who embodies this divine potential in its purest form, transcending the layers of physical existence to reveal the immortal spirit within. In this, we see parallels with the Hindu avatars, who remind humanity of its divine origin and potential for spiritual liberation.

The Son of God as the Perfected Reflection of the Macrocosm and Microcosm

In the ancient wisdom teachings, humanity is viewed as a microcosm of the universe, a small reflection of the vast macrocosm. The "Son of God" is the perfected human who fully realizes this reflection, embodying the cosmic principles within the framework of individual existence. Just as the universe holds the interplay of creation, preservation, and transformation, so too does the "Son of God" harmonize these forces within himself.

This triadic structure aligns with the Hindu trinity of **Brahma** (the creator), **Vishnu** (the preserver), and **Shiva** (the destroyer or transformer), symbolizing the cosmic principles within the human soul.

The "Son of God" is a living example of the alignment between the universal and individual, a bridge between the finite and the infinite, between form and formlessness. Brahma's role in creation parallels the emanation of divine energy into various forms, while Vishnu's preservation signifies the soul's inherent potential to maintain divine harmony within. This alignment is a universal process of spiritual awakening. Through self-knowledge and inner transformation, each individual can mirror the divine order and become a vessel of cosmic truth, as exemplified by the "Son of God."

The Christ Principle: The Activation of the Higher Self

The "Son of God" embodies what is often referred to as the Christ Principle—an awakening of the higher self within the individual soul. This principle lies dormant within all souls, waiting to be activated through aspiration, purification, and self-discipline. It is the light of Atma-Buddhi, the highest spiritual faculties of wisdom and love, energized on the mental plane. When the lower, desire-bound nature is transcended, the Christ Principle emerges, transforming the individual into a reflection of divine love, wisdom, and purity.

This process echoes the transformative qualities seen in **Rama**, who embodies dharma and the ideal of righteousness. Rama's unwavering dedication to virtue and duty, even amid personal challenges, exemplifies the Christ Principle in action—the steady unfolding of divine attributes within the soul through disciplined action. Similarly, **Krishna's** teachings in the **Bhagavad Gita** highlight the inner awakening that allows one to transcend ego and align with the higher self. The Christ Principle, like the divine qualities of Krishna and Rama, is an inner potential waiting to be realized, a call to embody divinity through love, wisdom, and righteous action.

The Second Coming: The Integration of the Lower and Higher Self

The concept of the Second Coming represents the completion of the soul's journey toward union with the divine. In metaphysical terms, it signifies the moment when the lower consciousness is fully integrated with the higher self, a complete alignment of mind, body, and spirit with the divine will. This integration aligns with **Vishnu's role** as the cosmic preserver, who descends repeatedly to restore dharma whenever humanity loses its way. Vishnu's avatars, each adapted to the needs of the age, symbolize the soul's continuous journey of integration and self-realization across lifetimes.

As the soul ascends, the divine presence within—symbolized by the "Son of God"—emerges in its full glory, uniting the individual with universal truth.

This "coming" is the resurrection of the Christ Principle within, the awakening of the perfected state that resides in each of us. It is the culmination of all spiritual striving, the point at which the soul transcends duality and realizes its eternal nature, much like the cyclical reappearance of Vishnu's avatars to remind humanity of its divine nature and purpose.

The Messiah as the Living Breath of Truth and Love

The "Son of God," as the Messiah, is the embodiment of divine love and truth within the soul. This is the higher self taking birth in the individual, transforming every thought, word, and action into a reflection of divine wisdom. When the Messiah awakens within, the mind undergoes a radical transformation, becoming a refined instrument of the soul's highest aspirations.

In Hindu metaphysics, the concept of **Prana** (the breath of life) parallels the Messiah's role as the living breath of truth and love. Krishna, who declares, "I am the Self in the hearts of all beings," embodies this universal breath, an inner energy that animates and connects all souls. The Messiah, as the living breath, represents the fully realized state where the individual no longer acts from ego but as a channel of divine love and wisdom, uplifting all those with whom they come into contact.

Galilee: The Path of Spiritual Progress and Resurrection

The metaphysical journey of the "Son of God" is also symbolized by the concept of Galilee, a state of advancement on the soul's path. Galilee represents a level of consciousness where the individual has moved beyond the constraints of the lower ego and embraces a forward-looking vision of spiritual progress. It is a place of resurrection, a return to one's true nature after overcoming the trials of earthly life.

This state mirrors the Hindu concept of **Moksha** (liberation), where the soul transcends the cycles of birth and death to realize its oneness with the divine. In this state, the "Son of God" appears to the disciple as a guide and example of perfected humanity, inspiring them to embark on their own quest for spiritual awakening. Just as Krishna reveals his divine form to Arjuna in the Gita, the "Son of God" in Galilee represents a guiding presence that encourages the soul's ascent toward divine unity.

The Pineal Gland and the Third Eye: Instruments of Spiritual Perception

The pineal gland, often considered the seat of the soul, is another key to understanding the "Son of God" as an enlightened being. It is through this center, also symbolized by the third eye, that the soul perceives divine truth. In Hinduism, **Shiva's third eye** represents spiritual vision and insight beyond ordinary perception.

When the "Son of God" awakens this inner vision, he gains the ability to see divine truth, just as Shiva perceives the essence of reality through his inner eye.

This vision, which transcends physical sight, allows the "Son of God" to perceive the oneness of existence, connecting him to the divine source. Through this inner perception, the "Son of God" experiences the direct connection between mind, body, and spirit, uniting the finite self with the infinite.

The Lamb of God: The Divine Sacrifice and Transformation

The Lamb of God represents the ultimate act of divine sacrifice, where the "Son of God" willingly limits his own nature to incarnate within the world. This sacrifice resonates with the concept of **Yajna** in Hinduism, the sacred act of offering one's actions and desires to uphold cosmic order. In the same way, the "Son of God" incarnates to experience the human condition, becoming a transformative force within the material world.

Through this sacrifice, the "Son of God" exemplifies the transformation of the lower self, which must be willingly surrendered to reveal the higher self. Like Krishna's guidance to act without attachment, the Lamb's sacrifice represents the ultimate surrender of ego, paving the way for the soul's liberation and return to the divine.

Conclusion: The Son of God as the Archetype of Divine Humanity

In conclusion, the "Son of God" is the ultimate archetype of divine humanity, the perfected state that each soul is destined to realize. Just as the Hindu deities represent divine qualities that guide humanity, the "Son of God" embodies these universal principles in a human form, bridging the finite and the infinite. By understanding the "Son of God" as a metaphysical process, enriched by both Christian and Hindu symbols, we are invited to embark on our own journey, recognizing that within each of us lies the potential to awaken the divine essence and become a beacon of light in the world.

8th Entry

Archangels, Cherubim and Seraphim, Elohim: Guardians of Divine Wisdom and Higher Realms

Sons of God, let us explore the profound mysteries of the celestial guardians—the archangels, cherubim, and seraphim, Elohim —each embodying distinct aspects of divine wisdom, protection, and spiritual guidance. These beings are more than symbolic figures; they represent archetypal forces that safeguard the sanctity of divine realms and guide souls toward enlightenment. As we journey through their attributes and roles, we will come to understand the importance of each in the greater cosmic order and in our personal paths of spiritual evolution.

The cherubim, with their flaming swords, protect the sacred spaces of higher consciousness, barring access to the unprepared. The seraphim, dwelling in the secluded buddhi plane, symbolize the higher laws and the spiritual discipline necessary to transcend the lower mind. Together, they guide us along the path of purification, ensuring that only those who are truly ready may access the wisdom of the higher realms.

Let us explore these divine beings and learn how their attributes serve as reflections of the potential within each of us, guiding us ever closer to the divine.

The Role of the Archangels: Divine Messengers and Cosmic Mediators

The archangels are often described as messengers of the Divine, those who carry out the will of God across realms. They are channels through which divine energy flows, providing guidance, protection, and insight. Each archangel represents a specific attribute of the divine, a facet of God's light, and holds a unique role within the hierarchy of celestial beings. They serve as spiritual guides, urging humanity to embody divine qualities within our lives.

Archangel Michael: The Sword of Divine Will

Michael, the "One Who Is Like God," embodies strength, courage, and protection. As the divine warrior, Michael stands as a symbol of the power of divine will. His sword is not just a weapon; it represents the cutting away of illusion, fear, and ignorance. In our own lives, to invoke Michael is to invoke the power to stand firm in truth, to conquer our inner darkness, and to pursue a path of integrity.

Michael's role reminds us that true power is not found in dominance over others but in mastery over oneself. His energy calls us to rise above lower desires, to sever ties with limiting beliefs, and to align our will with the will of the Divine. In doing so, we become bearers of light, protectors of truth, and guardians of our own inner sanctum.

Archangel Raphael: The Healer and Restorer

Raphael, whose name reflects restoration, wholeness, and divine wellness, embodies the energies of healing, renewal, and harmony. His presence is a balm to the soul, a reminder that all wounds—physical, emotional, and spiritual—can be healed through divine love and compassion. Raphael's essence is not merely the restoration of the body but the healing of the soul's disconnection from its divine source.

In calling upon Raphael, we open ourselves to the transformative power of love and forgiveness, understanding that healing begins within.

His energy urges us to harmonize our inner selves, to let go of resentment, and to embrace wholeness. Through Raphael, we are reminded that health is the natural state of the soul aligned with truth, and that sickness is often a symptom of misalignment.

Archangel Gabriel: The Divine Communicator

Gabriel, the "Strength of God," is the divine messenger, the one who brings clarity, revelation, and insight. Gabriel's energy represents the power of the Word—the creative force that brings ideas into form, that reveals hidden truths, and that aligns us with our divine purpose. As the one who announced the coming of divine light in various traditions, Gabriel symbolizes the birth of higher consciousness within us.

Gabriel calls us to purify our thoughts, words, and actions, recognizing the creative potential of each. His presence reminds us that communication is sacred, that our words carry vibrations capable of creating worlds.

To embody Gabriel's energy is to speak with intention, clarity, and compassion, allowing our voice to become a vessel for divine truth.

Seraphim: Guardians of the Buddhi Plane and Higher Laws

The seraphim are known as symbols of higher laws, protectors of the buddhi plane, where pure, divine wisdom resides. In their role, the seraphim ensure that the lower consciousness—driven by ego, attachment, and illusion—cannot access the realms of higher understanding without first undergoing purification. They seclude the buddhi plane, keeping it sacred and untouched by the distortions of the lower mind, ensuring that only the highest, most refined consciousness may approach.

This seclusion symbolizes a separation between the higher and lower aspects of our being, a distinction that is essential for true spiritual ascension. The seraphim embody the fiery, transformative energy that cleanses and prepares the soul, similar to how the flaming sword of the cherubim guards the entrance to Eden. Their presence reminds us that enlightenment is a process of refining our inner nature, requiring a dedication to higher principles and a release from base desires.

For the Sons of God, the seraphim serve as a call to elevate our minds beyond ordinary perception, to cut off attachment to the material and egoic aspects of existence, and to embrace the purity required to access divine wisdom. In their fiery nature, they represent the burning away of impurities, preparing the soul for union with the higher self, the source of truth and divine knowledge. This is a journey that requires discipline, humility, and unwavering commitment to the path of spiritual purification.

The Cherubim: Guardians of Divine Knowledge and Protectors of Sacred Space

While the archangels serve as divine messengers, the cherubim are often seen as guardians of the mysteries, protectors of sacred space, and embodiments of divine knowledge. They are traditionally depicted as beings with multiple wings, symbolizing their connection to the higher realms and their role as keepers of divine wisdom. The cherubim stand at the threshold between the profane and the sacred, ensuring that only those who are pure of heart may pass.

The Cherubim and the Tree of Life In sacred texts, the cherubim are stationed at the gates of Eden, guarding the way to the Tree of Life with a flaming sword. This imagery is rich with metaphysical meaning. The Tree of Life represents the divine blueprint, the structure of creation, and the path to spiritual enlightenment. The cherubim, therefore, are not simply gatekeepers but also guardians of divine wisdom.

To approach the Tree of Life is to embark on a journey of self-discovery, moving through layers of understanding, truth, and revelation. The flaming sword wielded by the cherubim symbolizes the transformative fire of divine knowledge, a force that purifies the seeker and illuminates the path. Only by shedding ego, falsehood, and attachment can one pass through the cherubim and access the wisdom of the Tree.

The Cherubim as Symbols of Divine Duality and Balance

The cherubim are often depicted with dual aspects—human and animal, male and female—representing the union of opposites. This duality signifies the balance between masculine and feminine, intellect and intuition, action and reflection. In the cherubim, we see the archetype of wholeness, the integration of all aspects of being into a harmonious unity.

For the Sons of God, the cherubim are reminders that spiritual growth requires balance. Just as they guard the sacred, we are called to guard our inner sanctum, ensuring that our thoughts, actions, and desires are aligned with divine truth. The cherubim teach us that enlightenment is not a singular pursuit but a harmonious integration of our higher and lower selves.

Archangels, Cherubim, and Seraphim as Reflections of the Inner Divine

Sons of God, the study of archangels, cherubim, and seraphim is not merely an exploration of celestial beings; it is an invitation to recognize these divine attributes within ourselves. Michael's courage, Raphael's healing, Gabriel's wisdom, the cherubim's guardianship, and the seraphim's transformative purity all exist as latent potentials within our own consciousness. By meditating on these archetypes, we invoke these qualities within, awakening our own divine essence.

Each of these beings represents an aspect of the journey toward self-mastery. The archangels guide us through specific facets of spiritual development, while the cherubim and seraphim symbolize the ultimate goals of purification and integration. In embracing these energies, we align ourselves with the divine order, becoming reflections of the light and wisdom that permeate the cosmos.

The Journey of Transformation The path of spiritual awakening is a journey through the attributes of the archangels, cherubim, and seraphim. We must develop the strength of Michael, the healing of Raphael, the insight of Gabriel, the guardianship of the cherubim, and the purification of the seraphim to truly ascend. Each step brings us closer to the divine within, to the realization that we are not separate from these celestial forces but are indeed manifestations of them.

Conclusion: The Divine Archetypes as Guides and Guardians

As we walk the path of enlightenment, let us remember that the archangels, cherubim, and seraphim are not distant beings but aspects of our own higher self, beckoning us to rise to our true potential.

Sons of God, embrace these divine archetypes as guides, protectors, and teachers. Through their wisdom, courage, compassion, and purity, may you come to know the divinity within you, standing as guardians of sacred truth, bearers of healing light, and vessels of divine will.

The Elohim: Custodians of Divine Will, Masters of Ether, and Benders of Light

Suns of God, we embark on a profound journey into the mysteries of the Elohim—those divine beings who serve as architects of creation, custodians of cosmic duality, and guardians of the unseen. Far beyond symbolic representations, the Elohim embody the seamless interplay of divine will, light, and Ether, orchestrating the harmony of existence.

Their nature invites us to consider not only the cosmos but also our role within it. As reflections of their power and potential, we are tasked with understanding and embodying their divine purpose, becoming active participants in the sacred dance of creation.

The Elohim and Cosmic Duality

At the heart of creation lies duality: the balance between the spiritual and the material, the visible and the invisible. The Elohim, as divine creators and maintainers, embody this duality. They weave the spiritual essence into material form, harmonizing the forces that sustain the cosmos.

This duality is not opposition but a sacred interplay. Through their divine activity, the Elohim remind us that the material world is a reflection of a higher spiritual order. They are both the breath that inspires existence and the silent force that sustains it.

As Suns of God, we too are called to embrace this dual nature. The Elohim challenge us to align our spiritual and physical aspects, to see ourselves as microcosmic reflections of their creative power, and to become vessels of divine harmony.

The Ether: The Divine Matrix

At the foundation of existence lies the Ether, the omnipresent medium through which all creation flows. Described esoterically as the "Father Æther," this subtle and unifying force is the primordial ground from which all elements and energies emerge. Ether bridges the spiritual and material planes, enabling the unseen to manifest as the seen.

As the synthesis of the elements—fire, air, water, and earth—Ether serves as the ultimate bridge. It is the medium that allows light to travel, transform, and manifest. In its nature, Ether represents unity, reminding us that all separations are illusions and that existence is a continuum of interconnected forces.

The Elohim, as travelers through the Ether, are not bound by its limitations. They utilize this divine matrix to navigate realms and fulfill their cosmic duties, transcending space and time to harmonize the spiritual and material worlds.

Light: The Expression of Divine Will

Light, far more than a physical phenomenon, is the first expression of divine will—the medium through which creation unfolds.

As it interacts with Ether and the elements, light refracts, bends, and transforms, shaping the patterns of existence.

For the Elohim, light is both a vehicle and a tool. Their mastery over light allows them to guide its flow through the Ether, crafting the intricate patterns of creation. This bending of light is not merely symbolic but reflects their ability to reshape reality itself, aligning it with divine purpose.

The Elohim as Benders of Light and Shapers of Reality

The Elohim are supreme architects of creation, endowed with the ability to "bend light" and shape reality. This capacity symbolizes their mastery over the forces of existence, allowing them to guide divine energy through the Ether with precision and intention.

Through this mastery, the Elohim transcend the limitations of space and time, navigating dimensions to fulfill their cosmic duties. Their movement, described metaphorically as "L-shaped" or multidimensional, reflects sharp shifts in reality where divine intervention reshapes creation's flow.

This ability reveals the Elohim as mediators of the cosmic order, harmonizing the interplay of forces to sustain universal balance. For humanity, their light-bending ability serves as an archetype of spiritual potential, inspiring us to transcend limitations and align with the divine.

The Elohim as Vehicles of Divine Will

As vehicles of divine will, the Elohim act as intermediaries between the infinite and the finite. They channel divine intention into tangible form, crafting the fabric of reality with precision and purpose. Their work is not separate from the source but an extension of its essence, ensuring that cosmic harmony is maintained.

This role invites humanity to awaken to our own potential as vehicles of divine will. By aligning our intentions with higher principles, we become co-creators in the cosmic order, manifesting light, truth, and harmony in our lives and the world around us.

The Metaphysical Attributes of the Elohim

The Elohim, as cosmic architects, harmonize the elemental forces that shape existence. Each element—fire, air, water, and earth—carries spiritual and material qualities that the Elohim unite into a cohesive whole. Their attributes include:

- **Magnetic Force**: Reflecting divine love, the Elohim draw the scattered fragments of creation into unity, aligning the cosmos with the principle of attraction.

- **Sympathetic Force**: Resonating with creation's needs, the Elohim respond with compassion and guidance, teaching us the interconnectedness of all life.

- **Occult Dynamism**: Mastering the unseen energies, the Elohim challenge us to explore the latent power of our divine heritage.

- **Mental and Intellectual Force**: Illuminating the pathways of thought and reason, the Elohim guide humanity toward higher truths that transcend the material.

Through these attributes, the Elohim remind us of the infinite possibilities within ourselves. We are not merely physical beings but co-creators, capable of wielding these forces to align with divine purpose.

Traveling Through Ether: The Elohim's Divine Journey

The Elohim's ability to traverse the Ether reveals profound truths about existence:

- **Dimensional Navigation**: By bending light within the Ether, the Elohim navigate realms effortlessly, harmonizing the higher and lower planes of existence.

- **Fulfillment of Divine Will**: Their movement aligns with the divine will, ensuring the balance and order of creation.

- **Rewriting Reality**: Through light-bending, the Elohim restructure the Ether, altering the flow of creation to restore harmony and fulfill cosmic laws.

Their traversal of the Ether reminds humanity of our potential to transcend limitations. By understanding the principles of Ether and aligning with divine light, we too can navigate existence with clarity and purpose.

Elohim and the Suns of God: The Journey of Becoming

For the Suns of God, the Elohim serve as mirrors of divine potential. They call us to embrace the dual nature of existence, to align spirit and matter, and to awaken the dormant forces within our souls. By invoking their attributes—magnetism, compassion, wisdom, and creative power—we transform into living expressions of divine truth.

The Elohim guide us not as external masters but as internal archetypes, resonating with the eternal truths within us. They inspire us to rise above illusions, to see ourselves as integral parts of the divine plan, and to act as guardians of sacred harmony.

Conclusion: The Eternal Dance of the Elohim

The study of the Elohim is not an intellectual exercise but a call to action. Their essence is our essence, their purpose our purpose. As we align with their attributes and embody their principles, we become co-creators in the ongoing dance of creation.

Suns of God, let us embrace the calling to become vehicles of divine will, benders of light, and guardians of truth. In doing so, we step into our roles as reflections of the Elohim's divine glory, manifesting a reality grounded in unity, love, and wisdom.

9th Entry

Celestial Wisdom: The Zodiac as the Cosmic Path of the Soul

Welcome, Sons of God, to a journey through the celestial realms. Today, we delve into the great cycle of life, embodied by the Zodiac, a sacred wheel of twelve stages through which every soul must pass. Each segment of this cycle corresponds to distinct mental and spiritual qualities that illuminate our path from the Son of Man to the Son of God. Through understanding this cycle, we prepare ourselves to explore the metaphysics of the Zodiac, each of which mirrors these celestial stages within the human experience.

The Zodiac is more than mere astrology; it is a metaphysical map, a divine template that charts the soul's progress. It shows us how the Higher Self, veiled by the material world, must ascend through layers of consciousness to rediscover its divine nature. Each sign represents a step in this journey, a stage in the purification and realization of our true essence.

The Cosmic Cycle: Evolution and Involution

At its core, the Zodiac represents a dual movement of evolution and involution. **Involution** is the descent of spirit into matter, where the soul experiences density and limitation. It is the process of embodiment, where the divine spark cloaks itself in layers of personality and identity.

Evolution, on the other hand, is the return journey, the ascent from matter back to spirit, where the soul sheds its earthly attachments and reclaims its original light.

This cycle, echoed in the Zodiac, unfolds across twelve stages, each representing a unique aspect of the human psyche and spirit. Together, they form the archetype of the "Perfect Man" or the "Archetypal Man"—an ideal that we all strive to embody. By moving consciously through each stage, we refine our mental, emotional, and spiritual qualities, aligning ourselves with the divine.

The Twelve Stages of the Zodiac: A Journey of Mental Qualities

As we move through the Zodiac, we pass through twelve archetypal energies, each representing a distinct mental and spiritual quality. This journey is an initiation, guiding the soul to awaken to higher states of consciousness.

1. **Celestial Fire of Aries** – Aries represents the spark of divine wisdom and courage. It is the primal force that initiates our journey, a reminder of the soul's will to individuate and experience life in the material realm.

2. **Stability of Taurus** – In Taurus, we find stability and endurance. This stage grounds the soul, teaching us patience and resilience as we begin our journey through physical and mental development.

3. **Duality of Gemini** – Gemini introduces us to the concept of duality, representing the interplay between the higher and lower minds. Here, the soul learns to communicate, bridging realms and exploring the mind's creative potential.

4. **Nurturing Waters of Cancer** – Cancer signifies the emergence of the emotional self, teaching us the importance of introspection, empathy, and nurturing. It marks the soul's descent into the astral realm, where emotions and intuition come to the fore.

5. **Radiance of Leo** – Leo brings us to the stage of self-expression and individuality. It represents the divine fire within, urging us to shine brightly and to embrace the unique light of our own soul.

6. **Purification of Virgo** – Virgo is a stage of purification and discernment, where the soul examines its own motivations and desires. It is a call to refine our inner world, cultivating mental clarity and humility.

7. **Harmony of Libra** – Libra represents the soul's quest for balance and harmony. It teaches us to navigate relationships and seek unity, preparing us for the ascent back to the divine through the integration of opposites.

8. **Transformation of Scorpio** – Scorpio brings transformation through the confrontation of shadow.

This stage challenges the soul to confront its fears, embrace change, and transcend lower emotions, initiating a rebirth.

9. **Aspiration of Sagittarius** – Sagittarius embodies the soul's desire for truth and higher knowledge. It represents the drive to seek beyond the physical, to expand the mind, and to glimpse the mysteries of existence.

10. **Mastery of Capricorn** – Capricorn symbolizes the attainment of spiritual mastery. The soul begins to rise above the material, exercising discipline and integrity, forging its way to higher consciousness.

11. **Unity of Aquarius** – Aquarius signifies the stage of unity and universal consciousness. The soul realizes its interconnectedness with all beings, embracing collective wisdom and humanitarian ideals.

12. **Transcendence of Pisces** – Pisces is the final stage, a return to the source. It represents surrender, compassion, and the dissolution of ego. Here, the soul merges back with the divine, completing the cycle and preparing for rebirth.

The Zodiac and the Manifestation of Divine Qualities

The Zodiac is not merely a journey; it is an unveiling of the divine qualities latent within each soul. Each sign encapsulates an archetypal mental quality that is necessary for the evolution of consciousness. Together, they form a complete picture of human potential. By passing through these stages, we learn wisdom, love, resilience, and the capacity to transcend the limitations of the self.

The planets serve as celestial teachers, influencing the mind and shaping these qualities within us. **Jupiter**, for example, governs expansion and wisdom; **Saturn** teaches discipline and structure; **Mars** represents drive and courage; **Venus** evokes love and harmony; and **Mercury** nurtures intellect and communication. These planetary forces guide us through the Zodiac's stages, each amplifying the qualities we must develop to ascend.

The Archetypal Man and the Higher Self

The Zodiac reflects the process by which the **Higher Self** emerges from within the **Son of Man**, evolving through each sign as it refines and purifies itself. This journey represents the alchemical transformation from the ordinary to the divine. Just as the planets revolve in their fixed orbits, so too does the soul progress through the Zodiac's circle, ultimately achieving self-realization.

In the archetype of the **Perfect Man**, the twelve stages of the Zodiac converge, illustrating the ultimate unity of mind, heart, and spirit. This journey is one of continuous learning, where the soul absorbs the lessons of each sign, integrating them to form a complete divine being. By understanding these stages, we align ourselves with the celestial rhythm, allowing the Higher Self to express its full potential.

Concluding the Grand Cycle: The Perfected Soul

As we contemplate this celestial cycle, let us recognize that the Zodiac is a mirror, reflecting our own divine journey. It reminds us that each phase we experience, each mental quality we cultivate, is a necessary step in our return to God-consciousness. Every sign is a gate to a deeper understanding, a new way of perceiving and embodying the divine within.

The Sons of God are those who recognize and awaken to this truth, who see the Zodiac not merely as a pattern in the heavens, but as a guide for the spirit's ultimate journey from man to divine being. This lecture has laid the foundation for our understanding of this cycle, deepening the exploration we began with the twelve tribes of Israel and their individual qualities. In this phase, we continue to draw connections between archetypes and celestial signs, illuminating how each represents a divine attribute that guides us toward the perfected soul.

Aries: The First Period of the Zodiac Cycle – The Seed of Life

In the metaphysical framework, Aries represents the beginning of the zodiac cycle and the *First Period* in the cosmic journey of the soul. As the gateway to all that follows, Aries embodies the primal surge of existence, the spark of life that initiates the soul's descent into matter and begins the journey toward spiritual evolution. This period signifies the divine impulse to manifest, a movement that brings forth the latent potentials within the cosmos into active expression.

The Primal Spark and Sacred Fire of Creation

Aries embodies the sacred act of creation, the first movement of divine life into the material realm. This initial impulse represents not only the soul's birth into individuality but also the act of divine self-sacrifice. Aries is the cosmic pulse that awakens energies within the universe, guiding the Higher Self (the divine essence within) into its first steps toward self-realization. As the embodiment of fire, Aries carries the life-giving force that both transforms and illuminates, symbolizing the eternal flame that dispels darkness and initiates renewal.

The Martial Spirit and Divine Will

Ruled by Mars, Aries reflects the cosmic will and the assertive power of the Higher Self's desire to express itself through action and courage. Mars represents the force that shatters inertia, enabling the soul to break free from limitations and actualize its divine potential. In this context, Aries becomes the archetype of the spiritual warrior, embodying the courage needed to confront the unknown and take the first steps toward self-discovery. This energy fuels the drive to pioneer, create, and transform, allowing the soul to confront its fears and attachments in pursuit of higher purpose.

Cycle of Involution and Evolution

Aries serves as the gateway for the soul's initial descent into matter, symbolizing the involution process where spirit enters the material realm to gain experience and wisdom. This descent, however, also sets the foundation for the soul's eventual ascent, or evolution, back toward unity with the divine. Aries represents the interplay between spirit and matter, where the soul first encounters individuality and the journey of separation. This experience in Aries prepares the soul for the cycles that follow, where it will refine and integrate these early experiences into higher wisdom.

Symbolism of the Ram/Lamb and Divine Strength

Aries is historically linked to the Ram or Lamb, a symbol of divine strength and sacrifice. This connection signifies the Higher Self's commitment to bear the weight of material existence, shouldering the challenges of life for the sake of growth and evolution. Just as the Ram or Lamb represents the strength and purity needed to initiate life, Aries provides the raw energy necessary to begin the soul's journey through the material and spiritual planes. It signifies the beginning of creation, where divine energies are harnessed to initiate the journey of transformation and refinement.

The Fire of Aspiration and the Path of Pioneering

In Aries, the sacred fire is not just physical vitality but the fire of aspiration, the relentless drive to seek truth and understanding. This inner flame propels the soul toward greater knowledge and self-realization. Aries is the pioneer, the cosmic spark that initiates the soul's exploration of uncharted territories, both within the self and in the universe. This pioneering energy represents the divine impulse to expand and grow, urging the soul to transcend the known and reach for higher levels of consciousness.

Lessons of Courage, Individuality, and Divine Intent

As the First Period, Aries teaches the soul vital lessons of courage and individuality. Through Aries, the soul learns the importance of standing alone, embodying its uniqueness as an expression of the divine. Each step within the domain of Aries reflects a commitment to evolve, with each encounter serving to strengthen the soul's inner resolve and alignment with divine intent. This period instills the qualities of bravery, discipline, and self-reliance—foundational attributes that prepare the soul for its journey through the cycles of life.

Cycle of Transformation and Regeneration

Aries governs the cycle of renewal and rebirth, resonating with the process of spiritual regeneration. This regeneration extends beyond the physical, touching every aspect of the soul's being. In Aries, the soul is invited to confront its illusions and attachments, engaging in a journey of purification that awakens the inner warrior. This process transforms the soul, aligning it with higher principles and strengthening its commitment to the path of self-realization.

Aries as the Archetype of Divine Beginnings

Aries stands as the archetypal seed of life, the Alpha of the zodiac's cosmic cycle. In its highest expression, Aries represents the journey from unmanifest potential to full embodiment, guiding the soul's initial steps and promoting its return to divine oneness. Although Aries marks the point of origin for individuality, it holds within it the promise of integration and eventual return to the Source. Through the challenges and victories experienced in this period, the soul remembers its divine origins and its purpose within the cosmic order, empowered to face life's cycles with assurance and divine courage.

The Interwoven Energies of Aries and Taurus: From Divine Impulse to Manifested Form

In the cosmic cycle, Aries and Taurus represent complementary phases in the soul's journey, each contributing unique qualities to the process of spiritual evolution. Metaphysically, Aries, symbolized by the Ram or Lamb, initiates the journey as the first spark of life—the divine impulse that propels the soul into existence. Aries embodies the qualities of courage, individuality, and the fire of aspiration. It is the archetypal energy of beginnings, a pure expression of divine will pushing forward into the unknown.

However, this initial surge of energy must be stabilized, grounded, and brought into form to fully serve its purpose. Here is where Taurus, symbolized by the Bull, plays a vital role. While Aries represents the unbounded force of creation, Taurus offers the grounding necessary to shape and sustain that force within the material world. Taurus provides the soil in which the seeds of Aries can take root, nurtured through patience, perseverance, and a steady dedication to growth.

Aries can be seen as the divine "out-breath"—a forceful release of energy, intention, and potential—while Taurus embodies the "in-breath," a drawing inward that consolidates and gives structure to that potential. This interplay between Aries and Taurus reflects a universal principle: the transition from the abstract to the concrete, from idea to form, and from spirit to matter.

Together, Aries and Taurus reveal the importance of balance in creation. Aries initiates the cycle with a bold movement toward individuality and action, while Taurus tempers this energy, teaching the soul to harness, shape, and cultivate it into something enduring. In this way, Taurus complements Aries, grounding its fiery impulses and transforming them into sustained effort and tangible expression.

In the metaphysical sense, Aries and Taurus remind us that true creation requires both the will to begin and the patience to build. This relationship teaches that divine ideas must not only be ignited but also nurtured and cultivated if they are to achieve their fullest expression.

Thus, the soul learns to move with intention and persistence, integrating the energies of both signs to manifest divine potential in the world.

Conclusion: The Significance of Aries as the First Period

Aries, as the First Period in the cycle of life, represents the essential catalyst for the soul's journey through the realms of existence. It embodies the uncompromising force of initiation, urging the soul to confront the unknown with clarity and purpose. This phase is not merely a beginning; it is a foundational movement in the cosmic process, signaling the soul's entry into individual experience and the unfolding of latent potential.

In this stage, the soul is introduced to the principles of courage, self-determination, and directed will. Aries imparts the ability to face life's complexities with a resolute drive, grounded in the knowledge that each action serves a greater purpose in the progression of spiritual evolution. It is within this framework that Aries instructs the individual to move forward with intentionality, setting in motion the dynamics that will shape subsequent stages of growth and transformation.

The First Period is thus a reminder of the power inherent in origins—a phase where the latent qualities of the soul begin their journey toward full expression. In recognizing the role of Aries, one gains insight into the deeper structure of the cycles of life, understanding that every beginning is both a descent into the material and a preparation for eventual ascent. This period establishes the enduring foundation upon which the soul's journey toward fulfillment is built, embodying the archetypal impulse that drives the cycle of existence forward.

Taurus: The Divine Matrix of Form – The Second Period in the Zodiac Cycle of Life

Taurus represents the second period in the zodiac cycle of life, symbolizing the consolidation of the divine energy into physical form. It marks the first steps into material manifestation, where the Divine, after initiating the cosmic cycle in Aries, begins to anchor itself within the structural forms of life. This stage signifies the involutionary process, where spirit descends into matter, becoming the "Matrix of Forms." In this stage, Taurus embodies the foundation of creation, a point where ideas and divine energies begin to take on physical shapes and qualities in the material world.

The Bull of the West: Productive Energy of Buddhi

Taurus is often symbolized as the "Bull of the West," a representation of the productive energy associated with Buddhi, or the higher consciousness plane. This phase corresponds to the flow of divine potency into forms, bringing qualities that will later evolve within nature and humanity. The Bull, as a symbol, expresses the primal urge for creation, the divine drive to manifest beauty, substance, and stability. This productive power of Buddhi in Taurus is what gives form to the etheric seeds of creation, which gradually become visible phenomena.

Involution and Spirit's Descent into Matter

In Taurus, the spiritual journey is characterized by the descent of spirit into denser forms, embodying qualities and potentials meant to serve humanity's evolution. This "Divine Sacrifice" of the higher self willingly descends into matter, undergoing limitation for the purpose of nourishing the souls in their evolutionary journey. As the spirit accepts these boundaries, it enriches the material realm with divine energy, allowing for the formation of stable structures essential for life. This period serves as a grounding force, a cosmic womb in which the qualities that will be expressed through all forms in nature are established.

Symbol of Strength, Resilience, and Sustenance

The symbolism of the Bull or Ox in Taurus emphasizes qualities of strength, endurance, and sustenance. The Bull is revered as a source of life-giving force, a creature that carries the weight of creation and contributes to the stabilization of cosmic energies. This symbolism highlights the Taurus period as one where divine energy is not only contained within forms but also directed to nourish and uphold the world, providing an energetic foundation for all that follows.

Divine Manifestation through Desire and Form

Taurus is also associated with the interplay between desire and manifestation. The desires expressed in this period are not merely earthly but represent the Divine Will shaping reality. The ancient mystics saw Taurus as a time when the soul, through the forces of desire and will, learns to shape its environment, discovering the divine potential within the physical realm. This alignment of divine desire with earthly form underscores Taurus's purpose: to manifest spiritual principles in tangible ways, grounding the abstract ideals of the higher realms into perceivable structures.

The Sacred Role of Taurus in the Zodiac

Within the zodiac, Taurus is revered as the builder, the force that brings substance to the formless. In the cosmic story, Taurus serves as the "Womb of Forms," where divine potentials incubate before emerging into material reality. This role as the cosmic womb emphasizes Taurus's function in sustaining life through stability, growth, and continuity, embodying the patience and persistence necessary for the unfolding of divine will across the cycles of existence.

Taurus and the Buddhi Plane Connection

The Buddhi plane, or the higher mental plane, is where divine forms first take shape. Taurus, aligning with this plane, signifies the matrix in which all divine ideas find their initial manifestation. This relationship suggests that Taurus acts as the divine architect, setting the foundational energy patterns that will later express in lower forms.

As such, the energy of Taurus resonates with the spiritual blueprint for the material realm, grounding cosmic energies that nurture and uphold life's evolutionary journey.

Taurus's Relationship to Other Zodiac Signs

In the zodiac cycle of life, Taurus serves as a counterbalance to signs such as Scorpio, where the energy of transformation and renewal is prominent. Taurus, in contrast, seeks preservation, nurturing the divine forms before they are later transformed. This polarity is crucial for understanding the cycles of creation and destruction within the zodiac, as Taurus anchors the forms that will eventually be transcended or transmuted by signs of transformation.

Gemini: The Third Period in the Zodiac Cycle of Life - The Duality of Consciousness

Gemini, representing the third period in the zodiac cycle, embodies the concept of duality in human consciousness. This duality is expressed through the symbolic "Twins," which signify the interplay between the higher and lower selves—what can be understood as the contrast between individuality and personality. On the metaphysical plane, Gemini teaches that human experience is not singular; rather, it is composed of two centers of consciousness that exist within the soul, both of which are essential for navigating higher and lower realms of existence.

In the constellation, the stars Castor and Pollux represent this dual nature. Castor, embodying personality, is mortal and bound to the limitations of earthly life, while Pollux, representing individuality, is immortal, transcending temporal boundaries. This cosmic pairing illustrates the tension between the transient self and the eternal self, each providing different perspectives and attributes to the soul's journey. Metaphysically, Gemini guides individuals to reconcile these two aspects within, urging them to find harmony between the self that is rooted in material experiences and the self that seeks spiritual ascension.

The Path of Evolution and Involution

Gemini's place in the zodiac cycle reveals a unique metaphysical purpose: to balance the process of evolution and involution. Involution represents the soul's descent into the lower planes for experience, learning, and growth. Evolution, on the other hand, is the soul's return to higher realms, purified and enriched by these experiences. The energy of Gemini facilitates this dynamic, guiding souls through the oscillation between earthly desires and spiritual aspirations. This journey is not merely about growth but about understanding and integrating the lessons from both realms.

In this period, Gemini invites individuals to recognize the interconnectedness of the lower and higher mind. As souls evolve, they engage with these dual aspects, moving from the lower to the higher realms of consciousness. This cycle allows for the accumulation of wisdom, gained through experiences that reflect both the mundane and the divine, merging them into a holistic understanding of self and purpose.

The Soul's Dual Function: Healing and Perfection

The Gemini period in the zodiac cycle brings forth the lesson that true growth requires the integration of both individuality and personality. Individually, the soul represents a direct manifestation of divine essence—a timeless spark that transcends physical limitations. Personality, however, is a temporary aggregate of qualities shaped by earthly experiences.

Together, these elements form a complete, evolving self that moves toward perfection through each reincarnation or phase of life.

This duality is not just a philosophical concept but an essential component of healing and self-realization. Gemini symbolizes the union of opposites and the necessity of reconciling them within the self. This integration heals the fragmentation within, enabling the soul to transcend limitations imposed by lower consciousness and move toward wholeness. By achieving this, the soul aligns itself with the higher planes, embodying both wisdom and compassion.

The Role of Higher and Lower Selves in Divine Purpose

In the zodiac cycle, Gemini serves as a bridge between the mortal and the immortal, linking temporal experiences with the divine spark within. This alignment allows individuals to understand that every earthly experience serves a greater purpose in the soul's evolution. The higher self, symbolized by Pollux, oversees and guides the personality, helping it to evolve by integrating divine qualities into its mundane interactions.

This relationship between higher and lower selves illustrates the divine structure within human consciousness, as the soul uses each incarnation or life phase to refine itself. The mortal experiences of Castor, bound by earthly limitations, serve as a crucible through which the eternal essence (Pollux) shines, refining the personality and aligning it closer to divine purpose. This process is a reminder that both aspects are essential for the soul's journey, as each serves a distinct function within the larger cosmic design.

Gemini's Message to the Sons of God

Gemini's message to the "Sons of God" is to embrace and understand the interplay of dual forces within themselves. This period within the zodiac cycle encourages a recognition that both individuality and personality have roles in the spiritual journey. The higher self exists to guide, while the personality experiences the world in a way that adds texture and depth to the soul's understanding.

Ultimately, Gemini calls for the realization that self-mastery is achieved through balance and alignment of these dual energies. By harmonizing the mortal and immortal aspects within, individuals embody the fullness of their spiritual potential, becoming channels for divine wisdom and compassion in the earthly realm. Gemini teaches that growth, healing, and ascension come not from denying one aspect in favor of the other, but from understanding, integrating, and elevating both. Through this, the soul becomes a unified expression of divine consciousness, navigating the zodiac cycle of life with purpose and clarity.

Cancer: The Fourth Period in the Zodiac Cycle – The Gateway of Descent

In the metaphysical understanding of the zodiac as a journey through life's stages, Cancer occupies the Fourth Period, symbolizing a critical juncture where the soul takes a deep descent into the realm of matter and the astral planes. Represented by the Crab, Cancer embodies the protective qualities that safeguard the soul during this profound transition. This phase in the cycle of life is marked by the soul's initial immersion into the world of emotions, intuition, and subconscious realms, all essential aspects of the Cancerian energy.

The Symbolism of Descent and the Astral Gateway

Cancer stands as a symbolic gateway, a threshold through which the soul begins its descent into the material and astral planes. This phase represents a point in the life cycle where the lower mind is energized and activated by astral influences, drawing the soul into a deeper engagement with emotional experiences and the development of the subconscious mind. The descent in Cancer is not a mere fall but an essential stage in the journey, allowing the soul to encounter and explore its inner emotional landscapes. This immersion is necessary for the soul's growth, as it initiates an understanding of the complexities within the self.

Dual Gateways of Cancer and Capricorn

In esoteric traditions, Cancer is viewed as one of two primary gates: Cancer is the gate of descent, while Capricorn represents the gate of ascent. Through Cancer, the soul enters into the world of form, taking on the challenges and lessons of material existence. It is the portal through which the soul becomes bound to the cycles of experience in the physical and emotional realms. This dual-gate symbolism highlights the purpose of Cancer as a phase that enables the soul to develop qualities rooted in introspection and emotional wisdom, preparing it for the ascent that Capricorn will later facilitate.

The Influence of the World-Soul and the Cup of Forgetfulness

Within Cancer, the soul partakes in what might be called the "Cup of Forgetfulness," a metaphysical concept signifying the soul's immersion in materiality and its subsequent forgetfulness of its higher spiritual origins. This stage is a necessary "intoxication" where the influx of matter and lower consciousness veils the soul's divine awareness. The Higher Self, or World-Soul, reflects through the individual soul, yet remains partially concealed, guiding subtly from within. Cancer's association with this cup signifies the beginning of individuality's journey through material existence, where memory of divine origins becomes latent, awaiting eventual awakening.

The Inner Life and Nurturing Force of Cancer

Cancer is traditionally ruled by the Moon, which governs the reflective, nurturing, and protective forces within the astral and subconscious realms. In this period, the soul learns the value of introspection, emotional strength, and the nurturing of its inner life. Cancer's energy draws the soul inward, fostering a sense of emotional depth and cultivating the qualities of empathy and compassion. This nurturing aspect of Cancer serves as a formative influence, developing the soul's sensitivity and capacity for connection, qualities that will enrich the soul as it continues its journey through subsequent cycles.

The Fourth Period and the Matrix of Soul Qualities

As the Fourth Period, Cancer establishes the foundational emotional framework within the soul. Here, the soul begins to absorb and reflect the archetypal qualities necessary for later spiritual evolution. This period of involution into emotional and intuitive awareness serves as the "matrix" from which more refined aspects of the Higher Self will eventually emerge. In Cancer, the soul is given the chance to integrate these early experiences of feeling and emotion, forming a vital component of its individual character and psychic development.

Preparation for Ascent: The Purification and Temperance of Cancer

Though Cancer is associated with descent, it simultaneously plants the seeds for eventual spiritual ascent. The experiences encountered in this period prepare the soul for its ascent back to higher realms, as it learns to temper and purify its emotions. Cancer's role as a crucible of emotional and subconscious exploration lays the groundwork for the spiritual discipline that will be essential in the phases to follow. It is within this descent that the soul gathers the wisdom and resilience needed to withstand the trials of the material world, strengthening itself for the eventual journey of ascent in Capricorn.

Conclusion: The Fourth Period and Its Application in the Cycles of Life

Cancer, as the Fourth Period in the cycles of life, signifies a critical stage where the soul descends into the depths of emotional experience and begins to understand the nature of the subconscious mind. This phase is marked by the soul's encounter with emotional complexity and the necessity of inner reflection. Cancer offers the opportunity for the soul to connect deeply with its own inner life, cultivating qualities of empathy, nurturing, and emotional resilience that are fundamental to the soul's ongoing journey.

In practical terms, the energy of Cancer encourages individuals to delve into their inner worlds, to understand their emotional depths, and to develop a balanced relationship with their intuition and feelings. It is a reminder of the value of introspection and the nurturing of one's inner self, both of which are essential for holistic growth. Cancer imparts the lesson of emotional maturity, urging the soul to embrace its inner experiences as a pathway to greater understanding and strength.

Through this archetype, individuals are encouraged to honor the depths within, recognizing that true wisdom emerges from understanding both the higher and lower aspects of the self. Cancer, as the gate of descent, serves as a foundational step in the journey, preparing the soul to face the cycles of life with emotional integrity and a deeper awareness of its own inner truths.

Leo: The Fifth Period in the Zodiac Cycle of Life

In the zodiac cycle of life, **Leo** represents the fifth stage, embodying a transformative period on the astral plane. Here, the soul encounters and integrates powerful forces of desire that manifest through passion, instinct, and a strong sense of purpose. This period is a journey inward, challenging the Sons of God to recognize, refine, and elevate their inherent strengths.

Leo's Role in the Path of Involution

At this stage, Leo symbolizes a point of introspective descent where the soul fully engages with its internal drives. This phase, often described as involution, is not about ascension or rising beyond but rather about integrating deeper layers of one's being. Leo's energy guides the soul through the realm of desire, where the challenge lies in understanding and directing intense energies for self-realization. This phase invites the Sons of God to recognize that true strength comes not from domination but from aligning one's will with higher purposes.

The Lion: Archetype of Inner Power and Leadership

Leo's symbolic representation as the lion conveys qualities of courage, strength, and leadership. The lion's energy in the zodiac cycle inspires the soul to embrace both its higher and lower aspects, blending nobility with primal instincts. This symbol encourages the Sons of God to harness their inner power responsibly, transforming raw ambition into a force for positive influence. Leo teaches that true power is not found in mere control but in the compassionate and courageous heart.

In this journey, the lion becomes a reminder to honor the balance between strength and humility. It is a call for the soul to assert itself with dignity, to roar not out of ego but as an expression of divine purpose, inviting others to rise with integrity and light.

Leo's Role in the Heart of the Zodiac

Leo is often associated with the heart, symbolizing both the physical and spiritual centers of being. Positioned centrally in the zodiac, Leo radiates the energy of love, generosity, and the willingness to lead with compassion. For the Sons of God, this signifies the importance of heart-centered actions, where one's leadership is rooted in service rather than self-interest. Through Leo, the soul learns to unify passion with purpose, transcending individual desires to embody qualities that uplift the collective spirit.

Harmonious Energies with Neighboring Signs

In the cycle of life, Leo's passionate energy exists in dynamic relationship with the nurturing essence of **Cancer** and the meticulous nature of **Virgo**. Through Cancer, Leo absorbs lessons of sensitivity and care, grounding its fierce energy with emotional depth. With Virgo, Leo learns the art of discernment, refining its bold expression into constructive action.

This interconnectedness between signs reflects the zodiac's continuous flow, where each stage supports and balances the others.

Conclusion

The energy of Leo represents a transformative journey of embodying strength, courage, and love. This stage in the zodiac cycle challenges the Sons of God to cultivate a heart-centered power, leading with integrity and purpose. Leo's influence is a call to refine primal desires, aligning them with a higher path that serves not only the self but also the universal order. In embracing Leo's lessons, the soul progresses in its journey toward unity and divine expression within the eternal cycles of the zodiac.

Virgo: The Sixth Period - The Archetype of Purification and Service

Symbolic Essence of Virgo

Virgo, represented by the Virgin, embodies purity, humility, and service, mirroring the archetypal journey of the soul's refinement. As the sixth sign in the zodiac, Virgo aligns with the phase of introspection and self-purification, a period where the soul sheds impurities, prepares itself for higher wisdom, and embodies the metaphysical ideals of discipline, discernment, and order.

In its metaphysical context, Virgo is not just about purity in the moral sense but represents the purification of the Self (Atman), where the soul examines and refines itself to eliminate lower desires, preparing to ascend to higher planes of consciousness. Virgo's association with harvest implies the soul reaping the fruits of spiritual labor, gathering what is beneficial, and discarding what hinders spiritual growth.

Realm of Inner Service and Duty

The archetype of Virgo, associated with service, reflects the soul's duty to refine and perfect its being. This service is not directed outwardly in material labor but inwardly as a dedication to the path of spiritual ascension. Virgo's energy suggests a devotion to the Divine or the archetypal Self by maintaining clarity, purity, and alignment with higher ideals.

Virgo's role in the metaphysical journey is the preparation and cultivation of the inner temple, which means aligning the soul with the virtues of humility, selflessness, and dedication to the greater good. This aligns with the role of the Archetypal Man or the Higher Self, as the soul progressively aligns itself with divine will.

The Earth Element and Its Implications

Being an earth sign, Virgo's energies are grounded in the material realm, focusing on the practical aspects of spiritual embodiment. This grounded nature reflects the soul's need to perfect its interaction with the physical world. Virgo's connection to earth teaches that true spiritual growth is achieved not by renunciation of the world but by engaging with it consciously, transforming every act into an act of devotion.

Metaphysically, Virgo's earth element represents the refinement of matter itself, aligning with the concept of involution, where Spirit descends into Matter to infuse it with divine purpose, thus beginning the sacred work of transforming the physical into the spiritual.

The Archetypal Virgin and Divine Wisdom

The symbol of the Virgin in Virgo signifies the untainted and original nature of the soul, which is neither corrupted by the ego nor bound by the desires of the lower mind (manas). The Virgin archetype in metaphysical philosophy represents wisdom and the immaculate potential within every soul to transcend base instincts and connect with the divine.

Virgo, as the archetype of wisdom, aligns with the concept of the Buddhi plane (realm of intuition and divine wisdom). In this context, the soul in Virgo awakens its inner sight to perceive truth, discern falsehood, and thus refine its mental and spiritual faculties. Virgo's discernment reflects Buddhi's light, illuminating the path for the soul to advance toward higher truths.

The Principle of Discernment and Judgement

Virgo embodies discernment, the ability to distinguish between the real and the illusory, the enduring and the transient. In metaphysics, this phase of discernment corresponds to the soul's growing ability to judge actions, thoughts, and desires in alignment with divine law.

This aligns with the teachings on the Archetypal Man, as discernment is required for the soul's progression through planes of consciousness. In the Zodiacal framework, Virgo is where the soul must learn the difference between spiritual nourishment and mere sensory indulgence, strengthening its resolve to pursue truth.

Purification Through Involution and Evolution

Virgo's period in the zodiac marks a phase where the soul undergoes purification through both involution (the descent of spirit into matter) and evolution (the ascent of matter back to spirit). In metaphysical terms, Virgo is where the spirit refines the physical form, preparing it to ascend and connect more closely with the divine essence within.

The process of involution, signifies the descent of Spirit into the material, while Virgo's evolutionary phase represents the spirit's ascent, purifying itself from material attachments. Virgo's energy allows the soul to strip away what is unnecessary, facilitating a return to spiritual clarity and unity with the Divine.

Virgo's Connection to Divine Feminine and Healing

As a symbol of the Divine Feminine, Virgo's energy brings forth nurturing, healing, and care for the soul's well-being. Virgo represents the nurturing aspect of the Archetypal Self, one that heals and restores balance, ensuring that every part of the soul is in alignment with divine intention.

This healing aspect correlates with the womb of Māyā, where primordial matter is both formed and transformed. Virgo, therefore, becomes the "womb" where the soul undergoes metamorphosis, shedding the old self and embracing a purer, more enlightened existence.

Virgo in the Cycle of Life: Self-Mastery

As the sixth period, Virgo marks a transitional point in the zodiac cycle, symbolizing a necessary phase of self-mastery. This period is the soul's rehearsal of self-governance, where it learns to maintain order, clarity, and purity amidst the distractions of the material world.

The emphasis on self-mastery aligns with Virgo's dedication to structure and discipline. Here, the soul becomes adept at controlling lower impulses and attunes itself to the guidance of the Higher Self, echoing the archetype of the disciplined seeker who diligently works toward spiritual liberation.

Virgo's Influence on the Physical and Astral Planes

Virgo's meticulous nature is also reflective of the physical and astral planes, where the soul learns to purify desires and master physical needs. On these planes, Virgo teaches the soul how to maintain spiritual cleanliness even while engaging with the physical world.

This aligns with the purification rituals that are symbolic of preparing the body and mind as sacred vessels. Virgo's influence in this context guides the soul to see the body not as an obstacle but as a tool for spiritual refinement, using earthly experiences to achieve divine clarity.

Metaphysical Correlation with the Archetypal Divine

In the archetype of Virgo, we see the mirrored image of the archetypal Divine, who is continually involved in the cosmic process of maintaining balance, order, and alignment. Virgo represents the meticulous hand of the Divine, ensuring that creation remains in harmony.

This reflects the role of the divine as described in the concept of the Archetypal Man, wherein the human, as a microcosm of the universe, mirrors this divine order within. The soul in Virgo seeks to embody this order, aspiring to reflect the perfection of the Archetypal Man through a life of purity, service, and spiritual dedication.

In summary, Virgo's metaphysical profile is a powerful representation of purification, self-mastery, and inner service. As the sixth period in the zodiac, Virgo aligns with the archetype of the Virgin and embodies the virtues of discernment, dedication, and healing. It is the period where the soul, like a wise caretaker, prepares itself for higher states of consciousness by purging itself of impurities and aligning with divine order. In Virgo, the soul learns to serve its higher purpose, not through grand gestures but through the humble act of perfecting the self. This prepares the soul to ascend, ultimately merging with the Divine through disciplined and purified existence.

Libra: The Balancer of the Zodiac and the Seventh Period in the Zodiac Cycle of Life

Libra represents the equilibrium point in the zodiac, symbolizing the shift from the inward process of involution to the outward journey of evolution. It stands at the threshold where the soul begins to balance the qualities it has internalized, marking the transition from homogeneity toward the rich diversity of creation. Libra is the sign where energies seek to harmonize, embodying the spiritual principle of balance that allows all forces to co-exist in cosmic and personal equilibrium.

The Process of Involution and Evolution

In the broader metaphysical framework, Libra initiates the evolution process on the astral plane, following six cycles of involution where spirit descends into matter. This seventh period embodies rest and integration, a "day of rest," which serves as an intermediate state between the inward, grounding forces of involution and the expanding, diversifying forces of evolution. Here, Libra's role is to ensure that what was previously unbalanced or latent finds a structured, harmonious form to emerge fully expressed.

Libra as the Gateway of Balance

Libra's symbolic balance serves as the gate through which involutionary qualities evolve. It is not merely a passive balancing but an active process that creates an environment for growth and expansion, setting the conditions for the qualities of other signs to emerge in a balanced form. This process establishes the perfect conditions from which all future periods of development will emerge, allowing energies to evolve in alignment with divine intent.

Libra's energy stabilizes the cosmic forces, ensuring that each subsequent zodiac phase contributes constructively to the whole.

Metaphysical Implications of Libra's Equilibrium

On a spiritual level, Libra represents the soul's quest for equilibrium within the dualities of existence, such as light and dark, spirit and matter, self and other. It initiates a reconciliation process where these forces find mutual expression, leading the soul toward higher understanding. This balanced point allows the soul to perceive both inner and outer realities with clarity, cultivating a deep sense of peace and unity that transcends individual experience. Libra's balance brings forth the qualities of justice, harmony, and symmetry, not just in outer relationships but as reflections of inner cosmic order.

Libra's Role in the Archetypal Man

Libra, in the archetypal structure of the human journey, symbolizes the embodiment of divine equilibrium. This archetypal position reflects the point at which the Higher Self intervenes in the material plane, establishing balance between the spiritual and physical domains.

Libra thus represents the soul's commitment to evolve with both internal cohesion and external expression, mirroring the divine's own balance between creative potential and structured manifestation.

The Seventh Hour of the Tuat

In ancient metaphysical systems, the seventh hour of the night represents the start of evolutionary expansion from the close of involution. Libra aligns with this phase as a "first point of balance," symbolizing an equilibrium of all opposing forces. It embodies the principle that from rest and stillness springs forth dynamic activity.

Libra's role here is profound, as it is the transition from pure potential to diverse manifestation—a pivotal stage in the metaphysical journey from spirit into the realm of form.

Libra's Relationship to Other Signs

Libra stands opposite Aries, the initiator, symbolizing the complementary forces within the zodiac. While Aries represents the impulse to begin, Libra embodies the wisdom of measured progress. Together, they complete the axis of initiation and balance, with Aries pushing forward and Libra harmonizing. Libra's balance with Virgo, which precedes it, also illustrates the natural progression from inward growth to outward balance, as Virgo's preparation of matter transitions into Libra's perfected balance.

The Energetic Blueprint of Libra

Libra's energy resonates with the principle of cosmic justice, representing the harmonious movement of celestial forces that maintain order in the universe. This blueprint imprints upon the soul an intrinsic sense of balance, guiding it to navigate life's complexities with poise. As Libra governs relationships, its energy encourages the soul to cultivate harmony not only with others but also within oneself, balancing thoughts, emotions, and actions to reflect divine order.

Scorpio: The Eighth Period in the Zodiac Cycle of Life

Scorpio represents the eighth phase within the zodiac, embodying a powerful transformation where the soul delves into deeper, often hidden, aspects of existence. This phase signifies a descent into the subconscious, where the desire-nature takes precedence, guiding the individual through experiences that catalyze profound growth, renewal, and an inner transformation that allows one to transcend prior limitations.

The Generative Power and Desire Nature

Scorpio is closely linked with the generative function, representing the mental-emotional process of procreation and regeneration. This generative power is not merely physical but also metaphysical, signifying the soul's ability to recreate and manifest new states of consciousness. The concept of regeneration here aligns with Scorpio's role in facilitating a metaphysical renewal, where the old forms of thinking and being are transformed, allowing for the creation of higher mental and emotional states. This is the capacity to dissolve outdated patterns within the self and create new, enlightened perspectives that bring the individual closer to divine wisdom.

The Descent and the Path of Inner Liberation

In Scorpio, the concept of "descent" is a necessary journey into the material realm, where the soul engages with trials and challenges that catalyze its growth. This descent represents the soul's conscious choice to interact with the physical and emotional realms, offering it opportunities for profound transformation. Here, the soul is invited to examine aspects of its own lower nature, such as base desires, fears, and attachments, through which it learns the balance between worldly experience and spiritual purity.

The "descent" and subsequent renewal in Scorpio illustrate the journey of purification, a release from lower attachments that allows the soul to reemerge with wisdom and insight. This process aligns with metaphysical teachings on spiritual evolution, where each experience serves as a chance for the soul to reconcile with itself, shedding what no longer serves it to continually refine its consciousness.

The Iron Age and the Challenges of Desire

Scorpio's association with the Iron Age highlights the intense mental and emotional challenges present in this phase. This period is characterized by a heightened focus on the lower mind, where desires, ego, and attachments to the material world often overshadow spiritual awareness. In the Iron Age, humanity must confront the illusions of self, recognizing them as the veils that obscure one's connection to the Divine.

This stage reminds us of the Kali-Yuga—a time of ignorance and disconnection from higher truth—where the soul is challenged to develop wisdom and compassion from within. For Scorpio, this journey through the "shadow self" or the inner darkness is essential; it allows individuals to recognize and transform lower tendencies, ultimately aligning with spiritual truth.

Renewal and Scorpio's Role in Spiritual Evolution

The cyclical nature of Scorpio underscores the soul's journey through successive phases of inner "renewal." This renewal, rather than literal death and rebirth, represents the shedding of false identities, outdated beliefs, and limiting emotional attachments. As the soul enters a new phase of being, it gains clarity, deepens in self-awareness, and aligns more closely with its divine essence.

Under Scorpio's influence, each "renewal" cycle is not just a repetition but an opportunity for deeper refinement of the soul's essence. Through each transformation, the soul discards layers of illusion, progressively reaching closer to the purity of divine consciousness.

In metaphysical terms, this process is akin to a purification, where the soul continually transcends old limitations and aligns with the eternal truth of its nature.

Multiplying and Be Fruitful: The Scorpio Lesson

Scorpio's energy is connected to the divine instruction to "multiply and be fruitful," carrying a profound spiritual meaning. Here, it signifies the expansion of inner qualities, faculties, and spiritual insights rather than physical reproduction. Through Scorpio, the soul is encouraged to cultivate and manifest higher qualities—wisdom, patience, compassion, and self-awareness—each of which serves as a testament to divine growth within.

For the Sons of God, this period underscores that true spiritual growth is about transcending lower desires and redirecting energy from a self-centered state into something expansive and divine. This transformation resonates with the symbolism of the Phoenix, which metaphorically rises anew from its ashes. In Scorpio, this act represents the soul's capacity to move beyond previous limitations, continually expanding its understanding of divine love and unity.

The Scorpionic Pathway to Self-Knowledge and Spiritual Enlightenment

In the zodiac cycle of life, Scorpio signifies an introspective journey that encourages the Sons of God to examine and confront hidden aspects within themselves. This examination of the "shadow self" is essential, as Scorpio's path involves releasing illusions and identities that no longer serve the higher self. The Scorpio period teaches that enlightenment is attained through the recognition, transformation, and integration of these aspects, bringing the soul into greater alignment with divine truth.

Scorpio guides the soul toward realizing that all experiences, even those filled with inner challenges, are purposeful steps in the journey toward spiritual wisdom. This phase encourages individuals to harness their inherent power, channel their passions constructively, and align with higher ideals, ultimately experiencing liberation and empowerment through self-mastery.

Conclusion: Scorpio's Metaphysical Blueprint

In summary, Scorpio serves as a transformative period within the zodiac, marked by the themes of transformation, inner renewal, desire, and the quest for spiritual liberation. It is a sign that compels one to look within, confront the self, and emerge transformed. Through the experiences associated with Scorpio, the soul learns to transcend attachment to form, using its generative power to manifest higher states of consciousness. For the Sons of God, Scorpio offers a profound understanding of the journey of the soul within the zodiac cycle of life, emphasizing the importance of inner alchemy and the pursuit of wisdom, ultimately guiding the soul toward unity with the divine.

Sagittarius: The Arrow of Ascension – Unleashing the Divine Mind in the Quest for Universal Truth - The Ninth Period in the Zodiac Cycle of Life

In the metaphysical journey represented by the zodiac cycle of life, Sagittarius embodies the profound transformation of the lower mind as it aspires towards higher spiritual awareness. This period signifies an advanced stage in the soul's evolutionary journey, where the intellectual and instinctual aspects of the individual are refined through the guiding influence of higher consciousness. Symbolized by the Archer, Sagittarius directs its energy purposefully, seeking wisdom and truth beyond the mere material plane.

The Ascension of the Lower Mind

Sagittarius represents the process by which the lower mind—associated with basic desires, instincts, and earthly inclinations—is transmuted through conscious aspiration. In this stage, the "arrow" of Sagittarius points toward a higher aim, symbolizing the desire for spiritual understanding and divine truth. The lower qualities, often bound to personal ambition or base impulses, are purified and directed towards nobler pursuits. This symbolizes a shift from the ego-centered perspective to one that aligns with universal wisdom.

Higher Self and the Symbolism of the Horse

The imagery of Sagittarius often includes the figure of a centaur, part human, part horse, symbolizing the dual nature of existence—the earthly and the divine. Here, the horse represents the mind's strength and endurance but also its susceptibility to desires. In its higher form, the horse is a vehicle for the intellect, carrying the seeker towards divine knowledge. It must be disciplined and guided by the Higher Self, which embodies the spiritual intelligence transcending personal desires. This control over the horse signifies mastery over one's impulses, guiding them towards a higher purpose.

The Purification Through Wisdom and the Arrow of Truth

The arrow in Sagittarius is not merely a weapon but a tool of spiritual insight and truth. This arrow, sharpened by devotion and directed by intention, symbolizes the focused pursuit of enlightenment. It is aimed at transcending the lower self and reaching the divine target. In the metaphysical sense, this represents the soul's unwavering commitment to pursue spiritual goals, piercing through the illusions and attachments that bind one to the material world.

The Role of Apollo and Divine Light

In relation to the Sagittarian quest for truth, Apollo, as the Sun-God, is seen as the enlightening force that purifies and refines. Apollo's light is synonymous with divine wisdom, illuminating the path for the seeker. As Sagittarius moves through this period, it seeks the "sun" of higher consciousness to enlighten its path, dispelling shadows of ignorance. This divine illumination nurtures spiritual growth, perfecting the mind and preparing it to perceive the higher realms of truth.

Liberation from the Lower Nature

The journey of Sagittarius is one of liberation. By overcoming the impulses of the lower self, the seeker ascends towards a state of wisdom, where they are no longer bound by ego or illusion. The process is both a sacrifice and an elevation, where the soul releases attachments to the lower mind's desires, reaching towards the ideals of universal love, compassion, and understanding. This liberation is the ultimate aim of the Sagittarian cycle within the zodiac, aligning the soul with the divine order and integrating the higher spiritual principles into the individual's consciousness.

The Energetic Blueprint of Sagittarius

In this stage, Sagittarius serves as a blueprint for the alignment of human will with divine purpose. The energy of Sagittarius impels the soul to search for truth in all aspects, breaking free from limitations of thought and belief systems. It is a journey of expansion—both intellectual and spiritual—where the mind is stretched to embrace universal principles. The Sagittarian energy encourages openness, philosophical inquiry, and a boundless pursuit of knowledge that transcends earthly concerns.

Integration into the Divine Cycle

Sagittarius, as the ninth period in the zodiac cycle, prepares the soul for its final stages in the journey of spiritual transformation. It represents a preparatory phase where wisdom gained from personal experiences is synthesized into a broader understanding. By the end of this period, the individual is no longer driven by personal desires but is guided by a higher vision that serves the collective good. This integration aligns the soul with the rhythm of the cosmos, facilitating the realization of one's divine nature.

Capricorn: The Pinnacle of Spiritual Aspiration in the Zodiac Cycle of Life
Tenth Period in the Zodiac Cycle of Life

Capricorn represents the tenth period within the zodiac cycle, embodying the journey of the soul as it seeks to rise above material limitations and aspire toward higher realms of consciousness. Often symbolized as the mountain-climbing goat or as an elephant in certain ancient systems, Capricorn signifies the determined ascent of the soul toward spiritual wisdom. In this period, the Higher Self, represented by the "White He-goat," begins to transcend the constraints of the lower mind, climbing the mountain of aspiration toward unity with the divine.

The White He-Goat: A Symbol of Transcendence and Purity

The emblem of the white he-goat symbolizes purity and the soul's commitment to ascend beyond the worldly attachments of the lower self. Capricorn's association with the mountain or heights illustrates this sign's role as a spiritual climber. In metaphysical terms, this journey reflects the soul's progression from lower desires, symbolized by material concerns and ego-driven actions, toward the realization of divine truth and ultimate liberation. The white color of the goat also signifies the purity and clarity of consciousness that are attained as the soul continues to ascend, moving closer to its true essence in the divine realm.

Capricorn and the Element of Aspiration

Capricorn's energy is one of aspiration, a force that propels the soul upward. This energy acts as a bridge between the lower and higher planes of existence. In this stage of the zodiac cycle, the soul is in a transformative process, converting the lower aspects of mind and matter into higher understanding and wisdom. Capricorn teaches that spiritual evolution is not an effortless journey but one that requires discipline, perseverance, and inner strength. The act of ascending the mountain, or overcoming challenges, symbolizes the soul's commitment to its purpose despite obstacles and distractions.

Involution and Evolution: The Spiritual Significance of Capricorn

Capricorn plays a dual role in the metaphysical framework of involution and evolution. On one hand, it marks the culmination of the involutionary process, where the soul has descended into matter and has undergone trials in the physical and emotional planes. On the other, it marks the beginning of the soul's conscious return or evolution back to its divine origin. The soul, having gained wisdom from the material realms, begins its upward journey, aiming to reintegrate with its spiritual source. Capricorn thus serves as the turning point where the soul fully commits to transcendence, moving beyond the limitations of physical existence.

The Goat's Journey Through Darkness to Light

In Capricorn, the soul often encounters trials that test its endurance, integrity, and resolve. These tests represent the purification process, in which lower desires are transmuted and sublimated into spiritual understanding. The darkness of material challenges is transformed into the light of spiritual awakening, as the soul learns to master its environment rather than being bound by it. This transition from darkness to light is a sacred aspect of Capricorn's journey, as it teaches that through struggle and persistence, the soul can achieve spiritual clarity.

Connection to the Buddhi Plane: Capricorn's Higher Consciousness

Capricorn's metaphysical role is deeply connected to the Buddhi plane, or the plane of higher mental consciousness. In this context, Capricorn is seen as the energy that facilitates the soul's access to divine wisdom and intuition, going beyond the limitations of ordinary thought. It is here that the soul develops its higher mental faculties, bridging the gap between human perception and divine knowledge. Capricorn thus serves as the custodian of wisdom, guiding the soul to recognize and harness its own inner divinity.

Capricorn as the "Gate of the Gods"

Capricorn holds a unique position within the zodiac as the "Gate of the Gods," symbolizing the portal through which souls ascend toward divine realization. While Cancer, its polar opposite, represents the descent of the soul into material life, Capricorn represents the ascent back toward spiritual origin. This gate marks the soul's passage into higher states of consciousness, where it sheds the attachments of the material world and steps into a more refined state of being. Capricorn, therefore, stands as the gateway to liberation, offering the soul a path to transcendence and alignment with the universal mind.

Strength, Resilience, and the Capacity for Spiritual Endurance

The essence of Capricorn is one of strength and resilience, qualities that are essential for spiritual progress. The symbolism of the elephant and goat highlights the grounded yet unwavering nature of Capricorn's energy. Just as an elephant moves steadily and purposefully, Capricorn's influence provides the soul with a sturdy foundation from which to rise. This strength is not merely physical but deeply rooted in spiritual fortitude, allowing the soul to remain anchored in truth and purpose, regardless of external circumstances.

The Role of Capricorn in the Zodiac Cycle of Life

Within the zodiac cycle, Capricorn serves as a pillar of wisdom, endurance, and spiritual aspiration. It embodies the teachings that emphasize self-mastery, the pursuit of higher knowledge, and the commitment to one's spiritual journey. Capricorn's role is to ground the soul's journey, providing the stability and determination needed to reach the heights of spiritual realization. In the cosmic framework, Capricorn helps maintain the balance between the material and spiritual realms, offering the soul a pathway to ascend after learning the lessons of earthly existence.

In this period, Capricorn imparts the understanding that spiritual evolution is a continuous process of inner refinement. By embracing the qualities of Capricorn, the soul learns the importance of resilience, commitment, and the pursuit of divine wisdom, ultimately preparing itself to rejoin the source of all creation. Capricorn, as the tenth period, represents the gateway to higher consciousness, reminding the soul that true freedom lies in the attainment of spiritual knowledge and liberation from the cycles of material existence.

Aquarius: The Eleventh Cycle of Life

Aquarius symbolizes the eleventh period in the zodiacal cycle, marking a significant advancement toward spiritual maturity and the evolution of consciousness. Represented as the Water Bearer, Aquarius embodies the concept of the soul's capacity to channel divine truth. In this cycle, one is called to recognize themselves as a vessel of the higher truth, bearing the waters of wisdom to nourish and elevate the world around them.

The Element of Water and the Flow of Divine Truth

In Aquarius, water signifies truth flowing from a higher source. This cycle calls for alignment with the higher self to access and distribute this truth. Water, as an element, represents the boundless qualities of unity, purity, and comprehension. It is a medium that bridges the physical and spiritual realms, symbolizing both the wisdom that nourishes life and the higher understanding that transcends the ordinary. The Aquarian call is to allow this "water" to flow through oneself as a channel, recognizing that truth cannot be contained but must be shared, echoing the expansive nature of divine consciousness.

Spiritual Evolution and Inner Awareness

Aquarius reflects an evolved consciousness, the fruit of previous cycles where qualities have been refined and elevated. Here, the individual experiences a heightened state of spiritual awareness and an openness to the divine influence. This period signifies the awakening of the inner Buddha-nature or Christ-consciousness, representing wisdom that has risen above material limitations. It is a time to embody and express this wisdom not only for personal enlightenment but for the benefit of the collective.

The Role of Purity and Transcendence

As the Water Bearer pours forth, Aquarius emphasizes the need for purification—of mind, spirit, and intentions. This purification facilitates a direct connection with the higher self, enabling a clear outpouring of truth and compassion. The Aquarian journey involves moving beyond individual ego, letting go of self-centered desires, and embracing universal values. The water from the "fountain of truth" must be pure to fulfill its role, symbolizing the necessity of inner clarity and sincerity in one's spiritual path.

Integration with Cosmic Order

Aquarius signifies alignment with a universal rhythm that transcends personal agendas. The energies of this period encourage an understanding of one's role within the broader cosmic structure. This cycle reflects a stage where the individual's actions and thoughts are no longer isolated but are interwoven with the larger fabric of existence, promoting harmony between individual purpose and universal will.

Service as a Spiritual Practice

In the Aquarian cycle, service to others emerges as a primary expression of spiritual maturity. As one channels divine truth, they become a vessel for collective healing and enlightenment. The energies here promote an outward flow, moving from the self to the collective, affirming that the path of enlightenment involves lifting others along the way.

This profile for Aquarius serves as guidance for individuals within this cycle to cultivate and embody these qualities, aligning with the divine purpose and cosmic rhythms. Each stage in the zodiac offers unique opportunities for growth, and Aquarius represents the refinement of the self as a channel for higher truth, setting the stage for the completion of the cycle in the following period.

Pisces: The Soul's Final Journey to Divine Unity - The Twelfth Period of the Zodiac Cycle of Life

In the zodiac cycle of life, Pisces embodies the culmination of spiritual evolution and the transition into unity with the Divine. As the final phase, Pisces symbolizes the integration and completion of the soul's journey through the human experience. This period represents the merging of the lower self, rooted in personal identity and earthly consciousness, with the Higher Self, which aligns with the ultimate Truth and the Divine Essence. Pisces is thus often associated with the concept of redemption, as the soul ascends beyond individual struggles and limitations to achieve a profound unity with the source of all creation.

The dual symbolism of Pisces is embodied by the image of two fishes, one representing the earthly consciousness and the other symbolizing the spiritual consciousness. The presence of two fishes suggests the eternal dance between the material and the spiritual realms, where the lower nature seeks to unite with the higher. Through this process, the lower self is redeemed and elevated, finding ultimate fulfillment in aligning with the higher, compassionate nature that Pisces embodies.

At this stage, the soul transitions from the journey of personal growth and individual transformation to a higher state of cosmic consciousness. This path towards unity is often symbolized by Christ's journey, as Pisces represents the archetype of the "Christ-soul" — one that has transcended duality and returned to the universal love and compassion of the Divine. The energies of Pisces encourage a deep compassion and an expansive love that transcends individual desires, aiming for the well-being of all sentient beings.

In this period, the ocean, or the "Great Sea," metaphorically represents the boundless realm of Divine Truth in which the soul immerses. This ocean of consciousness is both the source and the ultimate destination of all souls, symbolizing the all-encompassing nature of Truth and Wisdom. The soul, having journeyed through various experiences and stages of development, is now prepared to dissolve the barriers of the ego, surrendering to the vast, unifying sea of spiritual reality.

Pisces and the Integration of Higher and Lower Selves

Pisces is closely linked to the concept of integrating the lower and higher selves, symbolized in various mythologies as the unification of dual aspects within a single being. This integration brings about a profound peace and a sense of completion, as the soul achieves harmony between its earthly struggles and its divine aspirations. The soul's journey through Pisces involves embracing both the joys and sorrows of human experience, using these as stepping stones toward enlightenment.

Through the energies of Pisces, the Sons of God are invited to recognize the value of compassion, empathy, and universal love as vehicles for spiritual ascent. Pisces teaches that true strength lies in understanding and embracing the interconnectedness of all beings. This recognition becomes the foundation upon which the soul ascends, allowing it to return to the Divine with a renewed understanding of unity and love.

Practical cyclic exercises:

Cycles of Time: A 12-Part Meditative Journey

Each month, focus on the sign's qualities, its ruling planet's influence, and the particular energies that emerge from this period. These meditations are designed to align your inner growth with the celestial cycle, promoting a harmonious connection with the universe and your personal evolution.

Aries (March 21 - April 19)

- **Theme**: Initiation and Self-Assertion
- **Meditative Focus**: Courage, personal identity, and independence.
- **Contemplative Questions**: How can I assert my individuality? What new beginnings am I ready to embrace?
- **Practice**: Meditate on actions that can boldly initiate growth, both in self-expression and in physical life. Embrace assertiveness and reflect on how to lead with integrity.

Taurus (April 20 - May 20)

- **Theme**: Stability and Sensory Experience
- **Meditative Focus**: Sensual appreciation, grounding, and value.
- **Contemplative Questions**: What brings me true satisfaction? How do I cultivate stability in my life?
- **Practice**: Engage in mindful sensory experiences and cultivate patience. Reflect on material wealth and spiritual abundance, identifying ways to ground yourself in your values.

Gemini (May 21 - June 20)

- **Theme**: Communication and Adaptability
- **Meditative Focus**: Intellectual flexibility and curiosity.
- **Contemplative Questions**: How can I communicate more effectively? Where do I need to be more open to change?
- **Practice**: Journal your thoughts and engage in mindful conversations. Meditate on the power of words, embracing adaptability in thoughts and interactions.

Cancer (June 21 - July 22)

- **Theme**: Nurturing and Emotional Connection
- **Meditative Focus**: Home, family, and emotional security.
- **Contemplative Questions**: How do I nurture others and myself? Where is my true sense of belonging?
- **Practice**: Create a sanctuary space for meditation and emotional reflection. Focus on family and self-care, examining ways to offer and receive nurturing energy.

Leo (July 23 - August 22)

- **Theme**: Self-Expression and Creativity
- **Meditative Focus**: Confidence, leadership, and joy.
- **Contemplative Questions**: How can I shine more authentically? What gifts do I have to share with the world?
- **Practice**: Engage in creative pursuits and affirm your self-worth. Meditate on your unique talents, embracing the joy of self-expression without ego.

Virgo (August 23 - September 22)

- **Theme**: Service and Discernment
- **Meditative Focus**: Order, analysis, and healing.
- **Contemplative Questions**: How can I improve and refine myself? What areas of my life need more organization?
- **Practice**: Develop a mindful routine and focus on self-care. Meditate on discernment, examining your thoughts and habits to cultivate inner and outer clarity.

Libra (September 23 - October 22)

- **Theme**: Balance and Harmony
- **Meditative Focus**: Relationships, justice, and aesthetics.
- **Contemplative Questions**: Where do I need more harmony in my life? How do my relationships reflect my inner state?
- **Practice**: Meditate on balance in all aspects of life. Focus on bringing fairness into interactions and creating beauty in your surroundings.

Scorpio (October 23 - November 21)

- **Theme**: Transformation and Depth
- **Meditative Focus**: Power, intimacy, and rebirth.
- **Contemplative Questions**: What aspects of myself need transformation? How can I confront my fears with courage?
- **Practice**: Engage in deep, introspective meditation. Reflect on cycles of death and rebirth within, releasing attachments and embracing personal evolution.

Sagittarius (November 22 - December 21)

- **Theme**: Exploration and Higher Learning
- **Meditative Focus**: Wisdom, freedom, and truth-seeking.
- **Contemplative Questions**: Where do I seek meaning? How can I expand my perspective?
- **Practice**: Meditate on openness to new experiences. Focus on philosophical or spiritual studies and seek broader understanding through learning and travel.

Capricorn (December 22 - January 19)

- **Theme**: Discipline and Responsibility
- **Meditative Focus**: Structure, ambition, and patience.
- **Contemplative Questions**: What are my long-term goals? How do I demonstrate resilience and integrity?
- **Practice**: Set intentions for disciplined action. Meditate on persistence and responsibility, creating plans for personal and professional growth.

Aquarius (January 20 - February 18)

- **Theme**: Innovation and Individuality
- **Meditative Focus**: Idealism, community, and freedom.
- **Contemplative Questions**: How can I contribute to the collective good? Where am I called to break free from convention?
- **Practice**: Engage in progressive thinking and group activities. Meditate on the power of unity within diversity, balancing independence with collective consciousness.

Pisces (February 19 - March 20)

- **Theme**: Compassion and Spiritual Connection
- **Meditative Focus**: Intuition, empathy, and transcendence.
- **Contemplative Questions**: How can I deepen my spiritual practice? Where do I need to practice more compassion?
- **Practice**: Meditate on unity with all beings and engage in acts of compassion. Reflect on your intuitive insights, strengthening your connection to the divine.

Integrating the Zodiac Cycle

At the end of each zodiac cycle, revisit your journey and reflect on how each sign's energies have contributed to your personal growth. This 12-part cycle allows for a full-spectrum approach to self-awareness and spiritual alignment, enabling you to cultivate a balanced mind, heart, and spirit.

In each cycle, understand that the energies represented by the zodiac signs are not merely external forces, but internal archetypes that are meant to be integrated within your personal consciousness. This framework is designed to help you align with universal rhythms, building an awareness of the interconnectedness between yourself and the cosmos.

By aligning each month's contemplative practices with the qualities of each zodiac sign, you are invited to progressively embody these attributes, creating a holistic journey toward spiritual maturity and unity with the greater cosmic order. This cycle offers a structured path for those seeking to align their inner evolution with the grand cycles of time and cosmic wisdom.

Appendix: Subtitles by Topic

- **Apostles vs Disciples: A Metaphysical Exploration** – Pg. 149
- **Apostolic Chakra Guide** – Pg. 153
- **Aquarius** – Pg. 312
- **Aquarius Practical Exercises** – Pg. 322
- **Aries** – Pg. 266
- **Aries Practical Exercises** – Pg. 317
- **Archangel Gabriel: The Divine Communicator** – Pg. 248
- **Archangel Michael: The Sword of Divine Will** – Pg. 247
- **Archangel Raphael: The Healer and Restorer** – Pg. 247
- **Cancer** – Pg. 280
- **Cancer Practical Exercises** – Pg. 319
- **Capricorn** – Pg. 307
- **Capricorn Practical Exercises** – Pg. 320
- **Cherubim: Guardians of Divine Knowledge and Protectors of Sacred Space** – Pg. 250
- **Cherubim and the Tree of Life** – Pg. 250
- **Cherubim as Symbols of Divine Duality and Balance** – Pg. 251
- **Christhood: Part One** – Pg. 225
- **Christhood: Part Two** – Pg. 231
- **Eighth and Ninth Discourse** – Pg. 50
- **Gemini** – Pg. 276
- **Gemini Practical Exercises** – Pg. 318
- **Galilee: The Path of Spiritual Progress and Resurrection** – Pg. 243
- **Hathor** – Pg. 72
- **Hetep** – Pg. 29
- **Imhotep** – Pg. 57
- **Integrating the Zodiac Cycle** – Pg. 323
- **Isis** – Pg. 96
- **Kali Yuga** – Pg. 5
- **Leo** – Pg. 285
- **Leo Practical Exercises** – Pg. 319
- **Libra** – Pg. 294
- **Libra Practical Exercises** – Pg. 320
- **Ma'at** – Pg. 36
- **Matthew** – Pg. 172
- **Metaphysical Implications of Dan and Ephraim's Exclusion** – Pg. 146
- **Nephthys** – Pg. 78
- **Nu** – Pg. 17
- **Osiris** – Pg. 112
- **Pisces** – Pg. 315
- **Pisces Practical Exercises** – Pg. 323
- **Primordial Abyss and the First Duality** – Pg. 13
- **Ptah** – Pg. 64

- **Ruben (Vision of Faith)** – Pg. 139
- **Ra** – Pg. 123
- **Sagittarius** – Pg. 303
- **Sagittarius Practical Exercises** – Pg. 321
- **Scorpio** – Pg. 298
- **Scorpio Practical Exercises** – Pg. 321
- **Set** – Pg. 90
- **Shu** – Pg. 23
- **Simeon (Obedience and Receptivity)** – Pg. 140
- **Taurus** – Pg. 272
- **Taurus Practical Exercises** – Pg. 318
- **The Christ Principle: The Activation of the Higher Self** – Pg. 240
- **The Cosmic Cycle: Evolution and Involution** – Pg. 260
- **The Divine Unfolding** – Pg. 12
- **The Elohim as Benders of Light and Shapers of Reality** – Pg. 256
- **The Elohim as Vehicles of Divine Will** – Pg. 257
- **The Elohim: Custodians of Divine Will, Masters of Ether, Benders of Light** – Pg. 254
- **The Ether: The Divine Matrix** – Pg. 255
- **The Five Electricities** – Pg. 155
- **The Lamb of God: The Divine Sacrifice and Transformation** – Pg. 244
- **The Messiah as the Living Breath of Truth and Love** – Pg. 242
- **The Metaphysical Attributes of the Elohim** – Pg. 257
- **The Spiritual Constellation of Apostles** – Pg. 150
- **The Twelve Stages of the Zodiac: A Journey of Mental Qualities** – Pg. 261
- **The Twelve Tribes of Israel as Mental Qualities** – Pg. 136
- **The Transition to Apostles** – Pg. 150
- **Thomas** – Pg. 166
- **Thoth** – Pg. 42
- **Travelers through Ether: The Elohim's Divine Journey** – Pg. 258
- **Virgo** – Pg. 288
- **Virgo Practical Exercises** – Pg. 320
- **Zebulun (Order and Stability)** – Pg. 142

www.ingramcontent.com/pod-product-compliance
Lightning Source LLC
Chambersburg PA
CBHW051146290426
44108CB00019B/2628